Radical Hospitality

Radical Hospitality

Transforming Shelter, Home, and Community
The Wellspring House Story

Rosemary Haughton and Nancy Schwoyer, with Kimberly French

Foreword by Chuck Collins

PETER LANG
Oxford · Berlin · Bruxelles · Chennai · Lausanne · New York

Bibliographic information published by the Deutsche Nationalbibliothek. The German National Library lists this publication in the German National Bibliography; detailed bibliographic data is available on the Internet at http://dnb.d-nb.de.

A catalogue record for this book is available from the British Library.

Library of Congress Cataloging-in-Publication Data

Names: Schwoyer, Nancy, 1937- author. | Haughton, Rosemary, author. | French, Kimberly, author.
Title: Radical hospitality: transforming shelter, home and community: the Wellspring House story / Nancy Schwoyer, Rosemary Haughton, Kimberly French.
Description: Oxford; New York: Peter Lang, 2024. | Includes bibliographical references.
Identifiers: LCCN 2024008515 | ISBN 9781803744261 (paperback) | ISBN 9781803744278 (ebook) | ISBN 9781803744285 (epub)
Subjects: LCSH: Wellspring House. | Shelters for the homeless--Massachusetts--Gloucester. | Human-service nonprofits--Massachusetts--Gloucester.
Classification: LCC HV4506.G56 S39 2024 | DDC 305.5/69209744--dc23/eng/20240315
LC record available at https://lccn.loc.gov/2024008515

The authors are grateful for the generous funding contributions of Jerry Ackerman, Jen Cohen, Susanna Dammann, Patty and Marty Doggett, Anne Gifford, Pixie and Robert Gillis, Nancy Goodman and Jim Gutstadt, Susan Gray, Deborah and Raymond Grimard, Mark Haughton, Nic and Pauline Haughton, Don Hommen, Rebecca Koch and Nubar Alexanian, Sister Margaret Leonard, Jackie Littlefield, Melinda Marble and Jay Cantor, Carol Provenzano, the Rev. Margaret Rose and Bill Curran, Jane Saltonstall, Margaret and Jack Scally, Alice and Tim Schwoyer, Stacy and Tom Shaheen, Susan Stokes, Leslee Shlopak, Kathleen and Mark Townsend, Kristi Voelkerding, and Richard Wilson.

Cover image: Nubar Alexanian.
Cover design by Peter Lang Group AG

ISBN 978-1-80374-426-1 (print)
ISBN 978-1-80374-427-8 (ePDF)
ISBN 978-1-80374-428-5 (ePub)
DOI 10.3726/b21625

© 2024 Peter Lang Group AG, Lausanne
Published by Peter Lang Ltd, Oxford, United Kingdom
info@peterlang.com – www.peterlang.com

Rosemary Haughton, Nancy Schwoyer, and Kimberly French have asserted their right under the Copyright, Designs and Patents Act, 1988, to be identified as Authors of this Work.

All rights reserved.
All parts of this publication are protected by copyright.
Any utilisation outside the strict limits of the copyright law, without the permission of the publisher, is forbidden and liable to prosecution.
This applies in particular to reproductions, translations, microfilming, and storage and processing in electronic retrieval systems.

This publication has been peer reviewed.

We dedicate our book to persons of all ages who are working to find solutions to the poverty and injustice in our society and who know that the heart of their work is the practice of hospitality

Contents

List of Figures	ix
CHUCK COLLINS Foreword: Called to Something Bigger Than Ourselves	xiii
Introduction: Evicted	1
CHAPTER 1 Change Your Life	7
CHAPTER 2 Loving and Living	19
CHAPTER 3 Finding a Home	33
CHAPTER 4 Homemaking	49
CHAPTER 5 Stretching Hospitality	61
CHAPTER 6 Housing Should Be a Right	79
CHAPTER 7 Celebration	103

CHAPTER 8
What Is Radical Hospitality? — 113

CHAPTER 9
Education Is the Key to the Transformation of Poverty — 127

CHAPTER 10
A Community Ecosystem — 149

CHAPTER 11
The Lights Go Out — 165

Epilogue: The Power of Mutuality — 187

Bibliography — 195

About the Authors — 205

Figures

Figure 1:   All of us living together at Wellspring House gathered in front of the huge walk-in hearth on the September day Marygrace McCullough was married in 1984. Standing, left to right, are cofounders Jenny Richards, Rosemary Haughton, Nancy Schwoyer, Paul and Mary Jane Veronese. In the front row are Sissy LaVoie, Mark Baker (who joined us in 1982), and Marygrace. She wore the wedding gown that Rosemary made for her, the only item saved from a fire in our room, the whole day.   96

Figure 2:   Our first guest, Ellen Kelly, arrived on December 8, 1981, traumatized after a fire destroyed the building where she had a room in exchange for running errands for an elderly man. Raised in foster care since birth, she moved into an apartment in our first affordable-housing venture four years later, giving her the comfort and security of her own place for the first time in her life.   97

Figure 3:   Between 1983 and 1987 Shirley and Ron, a couple who had met and spent years at a state mental-health hospital, were our weekend guests, sleeping on the foldout couch on the sunporch. In the 1980s institutions across the country began discharging patients into "community care," often with no more than $20 in their pockets. But the community-living services envisioned by the advocates of deinstitutionalization largely did not exist yet. People with mental disabilities and challenges often ended up on the streets.   98

Figure 4: Board member Barbara Simpson was a powerhouse. Growing up poor and orphaned, she got an engineering degree and ran her own successful cabinetmaking business. Jumping on a chair at a board meeting in the early 1990s, Barbara inspired us to launch a $1 million capital campaign for a new education center and other needs, despite a down economy and two other big capital campaigns going on in town. 99

Figure 5: From the moment Ann Louise Gilligan and Katherine Zappone spontaneously showed up at the Wellspring House door our first year, they became our dearest friends and soul mates in our shared mission of empowering women to break the cycle of poverty. Influenced by Wellspring House, they founded An Cosán, a sister organization outside Dublin, Ireland, that provided education for women in poverty. When we started our education center, we invited them to be our first Scholars in Residence. In May 1996 we raised a glass in gratitude for all we had learned from them. 100

Figure 6: Lena Novello (right), president of the Gloucester Fishermen's Wives Association, teaches Wellspring cofounder Sissy LaVoie (left) and development director Paula Flynn how to clean and cook underutilized fish in Wellspring's Fish to People program in the late 1990s. Lena, a formidable and respected presence in the city, argued at endless meetings and hearings against the federal regulations that decimated family fishing businesses in Gloucester. 101

Figure 7: In June 2007 Wellspring House board members, staff, and volunteers celebrated Rosemary Haughton (center, in red jacket), on her retirement as associate director and clerk, though she continued to care for her beloved gardens. At her sides are Wellspring cofounders Mary Jane Veronese and Nancy Schwoyer.

Figures xi

Planning for Nancy's retirement as executive director the following year, the board was clear that they did not want the kind of transition where the outgoing director clears her desk and disappears. 102

CHUCK COLLINS

Foreword: Called to Something Bigger Than Ourselves

I arrived at 302 Essex Avenue on a sunny weekday in June, just in time for lunch. My friend Pat, who worked for a state housing agency in Massachusetts, invited me to join her for a meeting at Wellspring House, a family shelter in the seaport city of Gloucester. Wellspring's leaders were interested in starting a nonprofit housing development organization. We were warmly welcomed at the door of a large wooden house that resembled an old-time tavern.

In my late 20s, I had spent a fair amount of time in shelters for people without homes, including several in Massachusetts. I had volunteered at two Catholic Worker houses, including St Joseph House on New York City's Bowery, started by Dorothy Day. There was nothing in my experience, however, to prepare me for Wellspring House.

About twenty people were gathered for lunch, seated together at solid wooden dining room tables, with tablecloths and fresh flowers. There was the smell of baking bread, simmering soup, and, through a screen door on a sunporch, a sweet breeze coming off the Atlantic.

I joined the diners, enjoying delicious soup, homemade bread, and salad with a few early vegetables from the garden. I was introduced around the table. *Who were the residents, and who were the staff? Who were the volunteers?* It wasn't entirely clear. Spirited children, excused from the table after asking permission, flitted into the backyard garden, playing together or sitting under a shade tree. *This is not your usual nonprofit service organization.*

We adjourned to a side room, sun pouring in through a sliding glass door, where I met with Rosemary, Nancy, and other leaders, talking to them about the movement of community land trusts creating affordable housing. They were well up to speed, not only about the importance of removing housing from the speculative market—but about the theological roots of a common land and stewardship traditions. They were also clear in their vision: *Operating a shelter is not a long-term solution. We will not solve the problem of homelessness and affordable housing inside a system where housing is treated as a commodity. We need to expand the supply of permanently affordable housing. What are the first steps?*

I returned many times over those years between 1986 and 1989 to help with the start-up of the Wellspring Community Land Trust of Cape Ann. I met with Wellspring board members, staff, and volunteers, guiding their committee through the process of incorporating a new housing organization.

I felt very at home at Wellspring. The organization where I worked, the Institute for Community Economics, was also unusual in the world of nonprofits. Influenced by the Catholic Worker movement, my coworkers and I lived in community, sharing meals, common work, a large garden, and a commitment to hospitality. After evening meetings at Wellspring, I would roll out my sleeping bag on the carpeted chapel floor and stay up late by the fireplace talking with Rosemary, Nancy, and a cohort of younger Wellspring staff and volunteers in their 20s. Forty years later, all of these people have become lifelong friends, including Mick and Toni, a couple of volunteers from Ireland. Today, Maura is my acupuncturist, and Kay is my daughter's godmother. I've visited Mick and Toni a half dozen times in Ireland and serve as trans-Atlantic godparent and way station to their four adult children on their travels to the States.

Wellspring embodied the values of radical hospitality, a striking contrast to the stiff arm's-length culture of most nonprofit charities and "homeless service organizations" that were proliferating in the 1980s. *Radical hospitality* is not the friendly greeting you might experience at the hotel counter by a person trained in the "hospitality industry." Nor is it hosting friends for a meal and a bed, though there is something essential about creating conditions where friends and visitors "feel at home." At its essence, radical hospitality is welcoming the stranger and engaging personally and directly in the works of justice.

The founders of Wellspring House welcomed many people into their home, making themselves vulnerable to the struggles of adults and children at very difficult moments in their lives. By putting reciprocity and mutuality at the center of Wellspring House, the founders opened themselves to new relationships, risked being emotionally moved, transformed, inconvenienced, and subjected to new ideas and situations.

More than providing shelter and food, Wellspring offered healing, respite, acceptance, safety, and a pathway to stability. At its core was homemaking and a culture of celebration and imagination. In these pages, you will learn of the rituals woven into their shared life, the blessings, songs, prayers, and events like the annual women's solstice gathering. As Rosemary and Nancy write here, "Homemaking was the ground on which the whole mission of social justice would grow, in a space fit for human beings. Our idea of hospitality was not just having friends to dinner but a moral imperative, a work of justice, responding to our outrage at a system that regarded poverty and homelessness as acceptable."

In fostering a culture of "Power With" rather than "Power Over," Wellspring's founders began to break apart the patriarchal dualisms that divided people. In traditional service organizations, trained professionals are advised not to get too close to one's clients but rather to maintain professional boundaries. Of course, some boundaries are necessary to ensure respect and safety. Wellspring made the decision early on that they were not equipped to offer hospitality to people with drug or alcohol addiction. Yet here were people living alongside their guests, those facing troubles and setbacks in their lives. The divisions were blurred between "clients" and "service providers," helper and helped, teacher and learner, professional and volunteer.

Through this story, you will understand how Wellspring's founders, pooling their common resources and throwing their lot together, touched thousands of people. Their decision to change their lives inspired others and tapped a wellspring of mutuality, sparking the best of human spirit in form of volunteer energy, generous donations, and other forms of support for Wellspring's work. In some religious traditions, this might be called "grace," and in secular traditions, "deep solidarity." Either way, you will be hard-pressed to find another "shelter" where a former resident, relocated to stable housing but faced with a terminal illness, asks to return to Wellspring House to die not alone, but surrounded by her community.

***

Four decades after the founding of Wellspring, our society is facing multiple crises: extreme wealth inequality, increased numbers of people without homes, acute shortages of affordable housing, loneliness, and compounding problems of addiction, mental health, and persistent poverty. Across the globe, we are witnessing forced migration caused by war, climate disruption, political authoritarianism, and poverty.

Those who will be fortunate enough to stay rooted will find migrants, refugees, and others arriving in our neighborhoods. Some communities will respond by erecting walls or policing to contain those in need, creating illusory bubbles of protection, turning their back on these compounding challenges. Others will want to respond compassionately, knowing our governments and nonprofit charities will be strained and unable to respond to the scale and gravity of the problems.

Alongside these rising needs, there are younger people who both need affordable housing themselves and long for a deeper sense of meaning and community. The pathway for those who want to live a life of service is to work in the nonprofit sector, operating largely within "Power Over" culture, sustained by a charity system that is lacking in justice.

There are many, young and old, who are hungry for something that is rarely on the menu. They are eager to be of use, called to something bigger than a life of atomized living, isolation, excessive consumption, and work without meaning. There are younger people trapped by debt, pursuing educational training and jobs that leave them longing to align their lives with values of community, simplicity, sustainability, solidarity, and justice. There are older people, eager to share their gifts, seeking a deeper web of mutuality.

The Wellspring model of radical hospitality offers an alternative. People coming together, meeting their own needs through community, pooling what they have, committing to the works of mercy and justice as they are able. Within this book are lessons for emerging experimenters. It is also a cautionary tale about the risks of accepting government funds, creating traditional nonprofit governance systems, and bringing in consultants with cookie-cutter remedies that are not rooted in justice traditions. What happened to the founders of Wellspring reflects how fragile our shared endeavors can be, how easily and quickly people default to traditional organizational structures and systems, and ways of operating.

The Wellspring story of radical hospitality started with a powerful question, the discussion query that brought the founders of Wellspring together: "If you could change your life right now, how would you change it?" For readers who long for something more, something deeper, more connected and rooted, you will find here stories and inspiration for your journey.

Introduction: Evicted

Six years ago we were evicted from our home. It wasn't just our home. It was also our life's work, and it was the heart of the community we had created. The news came in an email, followed by a registered letter from the board of the organization we had founded and run for decades. We had four weeks to move out. Seeing our lives and our memories—all our books, pictures, files, records, and even our bits of crockery packed into boxes, brought out to the curb, leaving bare the rooms where we had lived for thirty-seven years—was devastating.

In the early 1980s we were part of a group of seven people who had a simple but radical idea: We wanted to live together and share our home with people in crisis who needed one. That was the beginning of Wellspring House in Gloucester, Massachusetts.

Most of us were well into midlife. We weren't satisfied by the work we were doing. We had sought community, mostly through our religious lives, but we weren't satisfied by that either. We chafed against the hierarchical systems that ordered our lives, in corporate, government, and even non-profit jobs, as well as religious institutions. Most of all, we were disturbed by the amassing of power and wealth that was creating an underclass we could see growing in our own city, a class system that shoved people to a bottom they could never climb out of.

We still hear these rumblings in conversations with people today, both young and old. There has to be a better way to live and work and thrive. There has to be a more just way to organize our society. But none of us can do it alone. We wanted to create and live in a community where people took care of one another.

The seven founders of Wellspring, five women and a married couple, gave up our jobs and homes. We took out two mortgages and worked part-time side jobs to pay them off. Over the years the two of us contributed about a quarter of a million dollars. We oversaw major renovations and additions, turning a well-worn eighteenth-century house into a welcoming home full of the aromas of bread baking, garden vegetables and flowers, and bright child-friendly furnishings, for more than 500 families who needed temporary shelter over the years.

Just as we were starting out, the Reagan administration slashed social support programs for people who were poor, while blowing up the national debt with military spending. For the first time in the country's history whole families, most of them headed by women, were on the streets or in their cars. The resulting explosion in the country's homeless population has been a permanent fixture of US society ever since.

The most important thing we did, even more than offering hospitality and shelter to people who needed it, was to create a community that practiced new ways of living and working together. We called it mutuality. We rejected the paternalistic handouts and stopgaps of anti-poverty programs, which had too many strings attached. Rather than calling in consultants to tell us what we should do next and how we could do better, we asked our guests. They were the experts in what they needed. We stretched to help them achieve those needs, one by one: by developing affordable housing, educating women to be change leaders, providing parenting support, and much more. Over the years our community extended far beyond the old wood-slatted walls of Wellspring House. We worked with organizations, agencies, and companies throughout our whole region of Cape Ann in Massachusetts, and we enlisted an army of mostly women volunteers and donors—thousands of volunteers, who found themselves changed too.

Most anti-poverty efforts seek to make their clients independent. Wellspring sought to create an interdependent community. We believe each of us is a human being with huge capacities and challenges, whether we're rich or poor, young or old, more or less educated, or have more or fewer abilities. In every relationship, sometimes each of us is the helper, sometimes the one needing help. Sometimes we are the teachers, sometimes the learners. We lived by the belief that generously living in an interdependent community is what brings happiness and also justice. Our biggest investment was in our community, not just the house.

Still, there we were. Evicted. Suddenly we were in the same situation as the families we had taken in over the decades. Most of them were homeless for one common reason. At the moment they had lost their home, whether because of eviction, job loss, fire, or domestic violence, they couldn't find another one they could afford. We weren't sure we could either, living mostly on Social Security at that point in our lives. And we weren't prepared for that. The irony was searing.

***

When the two of us were ready to retire, we spent a couple years working on a succession plan with our board to ensure that the essence of what we had created at Wellspring House would be carried on. For this, we did bring in consultants who really understood us. Committed volunteers brought their talents to the tasks of carrying out a smooth transition and a search for a new director. They created legal documents that specified how the property could be used and to ensure that we could continue to make our home there. As we now read over the research and advice on what's needed for successful nonprofit leadership transition, we can tick off the boxes of what we did: allow plenty of time, seek organizational development help, get infrastructure in place with the board.

Yet, the research also says, transitioning from founders to a second executive director is often tortuous. The new person often doesn't last. One study of nonprofit housing organizations undergoing executive transitions found that more than 70 percent went into crisis. Some don't survive. It can be painful.

Wellspring experienced the full force of that pain. The first candidate Wellspring offered the job to didn't work out. The board turned next to a candidate who had previously served in a couple of different roles in our organization. She knew what we were. And she had recently completed a master's in business administration and had learned many of the financial skills we had learned on the job. She was hired with the provision of making no major changes for a year.

Nine months later that new director announced that homeless families would no longer be welcomed and housed at Wellspring House, but rather in separate apartments to make them independent. Our comprehensive women's leadership program was shut down and replaced with training for high school diplomas and jobs. The board decided Wellspring would no longer develop affordable housing. The garden and clothesline were paved over for a parking lot. The mission statement was chucked out.

Within two years, nine program directors or key staff were fired, and another five resigned. Nancy was dismissed from her part-time post-retirement role as a fund-raiser and policy advocate, working from an office three miles from Wellspring House. She had to scramble to find health insurance by the end of the month.

Then we were evicted.

It was breathtaking how quickly what we had built over decades was dismantled. Wellspring House, once a home full of families bustling about their daily lives, was turned into offices for a typical nonprofit service provider, now managed from the top down.

**

What we helped create over three decades was extraordinary. Wellspring House succeeded and multiplied far beyond what we could ever have imagined, not just because of us. Wellspring was able to capture the dreams of so many people, from all walks of life, in the region where we lived. It left a legacy in the many community projects it helped create that are still thriving. It is a model that can be replicated still today.

There is a dream that persists in human consciousness, of people living together in companionship and trust, each person committed to the common good. It is a longing that lies behind all the social or religious experiments in history, large and small. The same dream that inspired us has empowered movements of protest and reform, such as the civil rights movement and even something as huge as the United Nations. In each case people come together, breaking the barriers they inherited to seek justice and compassion. That is the dream we followed and still believe in.

However, we all live in a society that has allowed ever-larger inequalities and injustice to flourish unquestioned. Nationally, homelessness is just as persistent and intractable a problem as it was in the 1980s. We don't have enough affordable housing, largely because we've never put the right public and private investments in place to create it nor named housing as a right. Our broken immigration system has failed both our own citizens and the increasing number of immigrants and desperate refugees fleeing war, violence, and weather disasters—adding to the number of people in dire need of compassion and hospitality. The wealth gap that alarmed us then has gaped ever wider, threatening to obliterate our middle class and splitting our society into haves and have nots.

At the same time, we see people all over the world rejecting the falsity that this is normal, joining their hands and hearts in protest movements and recognizing that there is really one cause to fight for, the cause of justice. Even as the powers of neofascism and racism try to define our future, that cause has galvanized all kinds of people: people of different classes, nations, and races, old and young, even schoolchildren, affirming that they don't want the old "normal" at any price. They don't believe in the hierarchies of power that have lied to them and robbed them. They will need to learn, as we did, to make decisions together rather than from the top down, which isn't easy, as anyone who has tried it can attest. Our goals can never be reached by the methods that actually caused the evils against which we are fighting. Top-down "Power Over" structures are designed to keep the power in the hands of the already powerful, as we have seen so often when liberators evolve into dictators. We were countering a powerful dominant culture and a powerful business model that rules even what nonprofits can do. Power, of course, concedes nothing without struggle. Evicting those who are trying to change the rules *is* the rule, but such evictions leave fractals with knowledge of a different way. And those will take root.

To challenge "Power Over," we have to demonstrate the effectiveness of "Power With" by creating communities of hospitality, places and cultures that welcome and include. That is what Wellspring House did. Other communities have done it as well, and we need more of them.

This book is called *Radical Hospitality,* two essential words. *Radical* comes from the Latin word for "rooted." *Hospitality* comes from a Latin word that means both "host" and "guest," or even "stranger." To practice hospitality, we aren't just inviting friends to dinner or to come for the weekend. We are making our life decisions, in the place where we live, rooted in an attitude of openness. Such hospitality is about saying "Come in," not only to people and ideas we know and feel comfortable with, but to strangers and even strange ideas. That isn't always comfortable, or even safe.

The story of Wellspring is a story of hospitality, its beauty and its dangers, its healing power but also its fragility. It is a story a group of determined people who tapped into their whole spiritual selves to create a public-facing organization that uncapped a wellspring of energy, common purpose, and generosity in a local context, and how that became a magnet for others to tap even more springs. We believe that this story is particularly relevant in our period of history, when the practice of hospitality, justice making, and community are desperately needed. That's why we need to share not just the story of destruction but also of the step-by-step creation of Wellspring House, a story of joy and wonder and luck and labor.

CHAPTER 1

Change Your Life

"If you could change your life right now, how would you change it?"

The question wasn't meant to be that challenging. It was an icebreaker to start off a study-group discussion at our church, the Catholic Parish of St Ann's in Peabody, Massachusetts, back in 1979.

Our group went around the circle.

"I would stop doing what I'm doing. I don't want to work for a big organization."

"I want to downsize my life."

"I want to work for a company that cares for its employees and makes a good product."

"I want to live in a community and share our home with other people who need a home."

"My husband and I have been welcoming young women in crisis to stay in our home, but I need support. We can't do it alone." That comment was from Mary Jane Veronese, who had for years volunteered with Birthright, the nonprofit that supports pregnant women.

People were nodding. This wasn't just an icebreaker. We all felt it. This was big. Most of us were in our 40s and 50s. We had already lived out decades, making decisions that we believed aligned with our values of justice and compassion. We were well along the paths where those decisions had taken us. But that evening, we were ready to consider major changes in our lives. For ten years we had already experienced radical changes in the Church of which we were all members.

Mary Jane had worked at General Electric before becoming a full-time mother and now coordinated the middle school religious education program at St Ann's. Her husband, Paul, had served in the Navy on submarines and used the GI Bill to get a college degree. He had taught high school English and worked his way up in the Peabody public schools to principal and assistant superintendent. They still lived in the house where they'd raised their daughter. It was bigger than they needed, and Mary Jane could have done without the pool. But Paul and Mary Jane both loved having the church youth group come over for parties and use it.

Nancy Schwoyer and Marygrace McCullough were nuns whom St Ann's had hired in 1969 to create a religious education program for all ages, unusual in Catholic churches at that time. They were hosting the meeting of ten people that night in the cozy living room of the little Cape-style four-room house the parish had bought for them to live in. It was their first home as adults outside a convent. They were thrilled to be able to host dinners for friends and family or for meetings like this one.

That night was the beginning of Wellspring House. We were all about to change our lives, radically. The four of us—Mary Jane, Paul, Nancy, and Marygrace—were among the founding group who within two years would open a house that welcomed people in crisis who had no home. It would be our home, too, not just a homeless shelter.

What we were feeling that night was similar to what we hear from people of all ages still today: We were compassionate people, often burned out, working too-long hours within the nonprofit or social-service structure; or working at jobs whose values we didn't agree with and doing the real work we wanted to do in our church or civic lives; feeling isolated or alone in our homes; trying to earn enough to keep up with the cost of living; without ever feeling we were making a difference in the world.

We still hear people today, asking just as we were that night: What do I want to do with my life? We hear young people questioning the expectations of them—going to college, getting a degree, taking on debt, getting a job and moving up the ladder in the hopes of paying it off and someday having a home of their own. They're asking: Is this really what I want to do? Many are deciding they do not. We also hear the question among older people: What do I want to do with the *rest* of my life? That was the question in our group.

Many in our group were also personally at a crossroads or in crisis. A man who taught our sixth graders was disturbed that General Electric had started manufacturing nuclear bombs, yet he needed his job there to support his large family. Another sixth grade teacher was counting on people in the parish to help her cope with a terrible marriage and to protect her children. Another was caring for a severely handicapped husband and an adopted son with serious learning challenges, while supporting her daughter's dream of going to college the next year.

Despite all that we were struggling with, together and privately, that night we got people asking themselves: If I could, what would I do? What was clear to us all that night was that we needed to keep talking about our answers to the question and pay attention to what they had in common.

We all wanted to practice hospitality. That word was key to the work we wanted to do. Hospitality meant opening our doors to people and also to ideas. We knew it meant risk, too. When you open your doors, you can't be sure who or what will come in. You sacrifice a degree of control. But you also gain new friends and breathe in a new spirit.

We had no idea then how far the next decades would outstrip those first imaginings. We could not envisage that Wellspring House would become a center of innovation and shared enterprise, on the vanguard of changing attitudes about homelessness, poverty, single mothers, feminism, and affordable housing. It would be a place of learning and discovery where people of all ages and desires could build their dreams. It would be a community that grew from decisions made together to create a place and an atmosphere that attracted people from all over the North Shore of Massachusetts and beyond. They would come not just seeking help but also bringing their own ideas and solutions on how to respond to injustice. We also could not imagine how hard it would be to ensure that spirit of community would continue when the founders eventually needed to step down and hand over the reins to new leaders.

***

At the time all of us were committed Catholics. Our faith and congregation were central to our lives. The changes we were about to make—to leave our jobs and homes and welcome people with no home to live with us—were only possible to imagine because an elderly pope decided to call a General Council of all Catholic Bishops.

The pope can call a council to deal with a major crisis in the Church. When Pope John XXIII was elected in 1958, more than a century had passed with no council. Many felt there was no need for one, as everything had been settled. The true one, holy, Catholic, and apostolic Church couldn't change. Because Pope John was elderly, many expected him to just keep St Peter's throne warm for a younger man. But unlike many previous Popes, he came from a poor family. His Church career had been in the diplomatic field rather than moving up the clerical ladder, like so many in the Vatican. He had watched with horror the rise of fascism. When World War II broke out, he organized the rescue of many Jews from the Nazis. He knew that change—big change—was essential if the Church was to serve a world that had experienced Hiroshima and the Holocaust. As he put it, the windows of the church must be opened "to let the winds of the Spirit blow through." When Vatican functionaries protested it would take ten years to organize a Council, his response: "In that case, we will do it next year." The council began on October 11, 1962, and over three years produced sixteen documents that outlined how to transform the Church from an exclusive institution of the faithful to an inclusive one that would welcome in and serve the modern world.

For many Catholics, like the members of our study group, the teachings of Vatican II were revolutionary and exciting. Suddenly the Mass was in English, not Latin. Instead of turning their backs to their congregations, the priests stood behind the altar and faced and greeted the people: "The Lord be with you." We responded: "And with you also."

But more far-reaching than any changes in our rituals was how laypeople came to understand the Church and themselves. The Church we grew up in expected us simply to "pray, pay, and obey." In other words, go to Mass and confession, support the church financially, and do whatever our priest or the church hierarchy asked of us. The focus was on the institution, not laypeople. Now we were being called to know ourselves as "the People of God," to discern where God was calling us to do the work of the Gospel: Feed the hungry, clothe the naked, welcome the stranger, love one another. Millions responded by embracing the new freedom to learn and think about our own spirituality and mission in the world, to teach others, to lead, and to act.

Not all Catholics welcomed these changes. Some felt shocked by what was being asked of them and hurt by the changes to familiar rituals they had put their faith in. Some clergy bristled at the loss of their previously unquestioned authority. Indeed, in the fifty years since, a powerful backlash has continually chipped away at the work of Vatican II. To our minds, the Church has become fixated on sexuality, birth control, and abortion, in a way that has nothing to do with faith, spirituality, and service—all the while covering up its own horrific sex abuses. For all those reasons, neither of us has identified as Catholic for many years and no longer feel comfortable going into a Catholic Church to worship.

But in 1979 we at St Ann's knew ourselves as Catholics free to ask questions, think for ourselves, answer God's call as we perceived it, and imagine and act on it. That's what we were doing that evening.

***

We had the good fortune to have as our pastor Father Paul Moritz, one of those clergy who early on "opened the windows" and embraced Vatican II. Father Paul loved being a pastor, and he cared for his people and listened to their concerns and ideas. He wanted the parish to be a true community, one that would meet the needs not only of its own parishioners but also the city, region, country, and world of which it was a part. He preached, for example, that taking action for peace was at the heart of the gospel. In one Sunday sermon, he expressed support for the Berrigan brothers—two priests who were jailed for protesting against the war in Vietnam. They had trespassed at a General Electric nuclear facility in Pennsylvania, damaged the nuclear missiles there, and poured blood on documents. Some in the congregation walked out before Father Paul finished preaching. Father Paul didn't just let them leave disgruntled. He knew many parishioners worked at GE in nearby Lynn, where nuclear bomb components were produced. Many didn't like what the company was doing, but they needed their jobs. Father Paul personally invited each of them to come talk to him, both about what he had preached, whether they agreed with him or not, and how to wrestle with the conflict between their responsibility to their families and their social consciences.

One of Father Paul's first priorities when he came to St Ann's was creating a first-class religious education program, for all ages. Prior to Vatican II, religious education had been mainly about teaching children.

In a program called the Baltimore Catechism, teachers asked a series of questions with specific answers, which students had to memorize: Who made you? God made me. Why did God make you? To love him and serve him in this world and to be happy with him in the next. This childhood learning was meant to be the foundation for life.

Boston College had developed a new master's degree that combined the theology of Vatican II with the education theories of John Dewey, Marie Montessori, and others who believed that people learn by doing. Sister Marygrace McCullough was the first person to receive the new master's in religious education in 1967. Father Paul asked her order to assign her to St Ann's, and Marygrace requested that Sister Nancy Schwoyer join her as codirector of religious education. As a former high school principal, Nancy had skills in program planning and budgeting that Marygrace welcomed.

Our task was to make adult education the centerpiece of the program, helping adults learn, deepen their faith, and realize their own mission in the world. We also trained more than fifty volunteers to teach classes for early childhood through high school. The two of us were part of the parish team and met weekly with the priests and deacons to make decisions and plans—not a typical arrangement for women or religious educators in Catholic churches. We were working out of mutuality, a principle that became central to Wellspring House. Father Paul also reached out to the community by starting the Peabody Interfaith Clergy Association, and it was Marygrace, a nonordained woman, they elected as their first president.

St Ann's set about challenging the Church's history of excluding people, even among its own members, women certainly, but many others as well. One evening Nancy was meeting with parents who were preparing their children for First Communion. Barbara, the mother of a teenager with Down's syndrome, snapped at Nancy: "Don't talk to me about community. When my Robin was seven, the priest told me she would never be able to receive communion. He said she didn't have to because she's already an angel and will go straight to heaven. That's pretty much what the other priests said each time I asked. I finally stopped asking when she turned twelve."

"I can tell you are angry and hurt by the way you have been treated," Nancy replied, "and I can't do anything about the past. But if you still want

Robin to receive communion, let's see what we can do now. I will talk to Father Moritz and get back to you. OK?"

Nancy went to Father Paul and told him she had an idea. The rationale for denying communion to people with mental disabilities was they couldn't understand its meaning. She would use the stained-glass windows in the church as her teaching tool to tell the story of Jesus and what the Last Supper meant, just as the Church had used them to teach illiterate people for centuries. She held a class telling the story behind one of the windows each week for Robin and Bob, another 17-year-old with Down's syndrome, whose mother Barbara had contacted. They asked questions and each took a turn retelling the story at the end of the class. The next week they repeated the story again and learned a new one. They loved telling the stories, especially to Father Paul, when he stopped in. He agreed: They did get it. They did understand that Jesus asked his disciples to eat the unleavened bread and drink the wine to remember his body and blood after he died and to remember the kind way he treated others.

On the night they received communion for the first time, Father Paul had the pair walk into the church with him, one on each side, right up the center aisle. They stood with him at the altar. He introduced them to the congregation. At communion time he called them back to the altar and shared the bread and then the cup first with them, then the rest of the congregation.

At the end of that Mass, Father Paul announced, "Now we are community. We've accepted Robin and Bob." The congregation burst into applause.

***

On the tenth anniversary of the adult religious education program, Father Paul, Marygrace, and Nancy invited the parish to reflect on three questions: How have the teachings of Vatican II changed you? How have they changed our parish? What other changes are we called to in the future? More than 100 adults signed up to meet biweekly in small groups. Our little group of ten people reflecting on how we would change our lives was one.

Just as those groups were starting in 1979, Mary Jane Veronese saw in *The Pilot*, the archdiocesan newspaper, that the author and lay theologian Rosemary Haughton was coming to Boston in November. Mary Jane came flying into Nancy and Marygrace's office. "Look! I think this is just what we need. Let's invite Rosemary Haughton for our day of retreat in November." Nancy and Marygrace had read some of Rosemary's writings and heard her speak at the Paulist Center in Boston. Rosemary was not a trained theologian but a laywoman and a married woman with twelve children, who was prolifically writing and lecturing about discovering God in actual relationships—parents, siblings, spouses, friends, community. She told the stories of people discovering the spirit among themselves, people doing the work of justice through hospitality. That was revolutionary in the Catholic Church, where we usually heard only from men, often not very interesting men. It was so exciting for us to listen to somebody speak about theology from the perspective of being a woman.

We loved the idea and asked Mary Jane to call Rosemary's agent, Margaret Kelley. "You're lucky," Margaret said. "She has just one slot left in her tour, before a month in Canada and then returning to Scotland for Christmas." We booked Rosemary for Saturday, November 10.

The week before the retreat was scheduled, the parish suffered a devastating loss. Carol and Dick Provenzano's 15-year-old daughter, Mary, died of leukemia. Week in, week out, since Mary had been diagnosed two years before, scores of people in the parish every day provided the family with meals, rides, and other care, including for Mary's younger three brothers.

No one who met her could fail to notice the light of Mary's spirit. During her last months in the hospital, Mary befriended a younger boy, Denis, also terminally ill. One day Carol called Nancy to ask: "Do you have the recipe for the bread for First Communion?" At St Ann's, children preparing for First Communion always came with a parent to the church kitchen to make their own bread together. Mary had been telling Denis about the meaning of the breaking of the bread and the sharing of the cup, and he wanted to celebrate his First Communion. "Wouldn't it be nice if he could make his own bread?" Mary asked her mother.

Carol brought in flour, a bowl, and a baking tin. Mary and Denis mixed and kneaded the dough, each with one hand because they both had IVs in their other hand. They baked the loaf in the kitchen of their hospital floor, and Denis had his First Communion. He died two days before Mary.

Carol and Dick held Mary as she died, on November 1. Her last words were "I've had the best parents in the whole world."

Everyone in the parish knew all this, and their hearts were broken wide open. Mary was waked in the chapel. The line to get in was a block long. Carol and Dick gave out the Communion cup at the funeral, packed with mourners, among them Denis's parents.

***

The next week the church hall was packed again for the day of retreat with Rosemary Haughton. The 100 or so people from the study groups formed into a big semicircle to listen to her stories about the early church described in the Book of Acts: People who broke bread in each other's homes as a symbol of sharing life together. People who welcomed gentiles and Romans even though it was against Jewish law to associate with them. People who sold their property to give to the communal group and took care of the sick and lame so that "there was never a needy person among them." It was exactly how Vatican II described the Church.

When the group broke for lunch, Nancy remembers watching Rosemary take slices of cheese, fold them, and eat them, one after another. She noted that they always must have cheese in the house in case Rosemary would come again.

Rosemary had given many retreats like this. She hadn't known about the Provenzano family and Mary's funeral the week before, but she felt an emotional openness and connection with the people in the room. During the afternoon, Rosemary asked that the tape recorder be turned off. She needed to tell them how she had come to a point of radical change in her own life.

She told the group about her husband Algy's alcoholism, a story all too familiar to women of many times and places, a story of genuine love and heartbreak, a story of pretending, compensating, covering up, protecting the children, and struggling to hold the family together. Algy's drinking had been part of his trying to cope with being homosexual, at a time when homosexuality was still a crime and poorly understood. When Rosemary and Algy got engaged, he had told her he was homosexual. Rosemary had grown up in the between-wars milieu where many of the artists, actors, writers, and others in her novelist mother's circle, such as Noël Coward, were known to be homosexual. In the culture of that time, it was possible for men to believe they could just choose to stop. They often got married and had families as a cover or a cure.

Despite all the misinformation, willful self-deception, and layers of illusion, the couple were genuinely committed to making a marriage and a large family. Algy got a job teaching English and drama at a prestigious and expensive boy's boarding school called Ampleforth College, run by Benedictine monks. The couple thought themselves wonderfully lucky. The school was academically excellent, set in superb countryside, and their sons were able to attend free as day students, riding their bikes to the school each morning. And there were friendly colleagues who also had young children nearby.

Less beneficial was the open bar in the faculty room, where teachers could help themselves any time and pay on the honor system. Most of their friends drank heavily as well. The culture around alcohol made it natural for everyone to tacitly ignore Algy's drinking. It got worse. The monks and others concerned about Algy acted only by picking him up from some pub or ditch where he had ended up, too drunk to get home. They did nothing to support him toward recovery. Rosemary often waited up for him to come home at night and had to get him to bed. She set up her own separate bank account to make sure the bills got paid. She didn't confront him for a long time either.

After every crisis, Rosemary and Algy kept talking and hoping, but nothing changed. The years rolled by, and the situation got more intolerable. Algy had three mental-health breakdowns. One afternoon, unable to face Algy's return home, Rosemary packed a picnic and on a desperate impulse set off across the fields with their youngest daughter by the hand. They sat under a haystack long enough for Rosemary to realize the utter futility of fleeing.

It became clear to both of them that the only real hope was for Algy to quit his job, and he did. It meant selling their home, and it meant telling their family of twelve children, including two foster children, what they were planning and asking for their help and support. Once the problem was out in the open and a decision was made, that last year in the job actually felt positive and hopeful. One of the best things for Rosemary during that whole troubled time in their family's life was helping out with the school plays, making costumes, painting scenery, even directing. In the final year Algy and Rosemary both helped put on a lavish production of "A Midsummer Night's Dream" that included youngest daughter Emma's appearing as the Indian Prince from whom Titania refused to be parted.

The shell of a plan had formed. They found, bought, and moved the family—not to a house, they couldn't afford one—but to three acres of field and woodland in southwest Scotland and a pile of logs, which the previous owners had planned to use to build a house. They had seen the positive effects that the hard work of carpentry, scene painting, and sweeping up had on the spoiled boarding students who had grown up with too much money and not enough love. And they wanted to build a community that would welcome and provide the same benefits to others. The whole family was involved in the plans, though some decided to stay in England in their own homes and jobs. Most of the children were by now young adults, the eldest already married.

The story Rosemary told the group was about taking risks. The idea was to form a hospitable community that would welcome others who needed a home and a community and a change, just as she and Algy had needed. The place became known as Lothlorien, named after the magical woodland kingdom in Tolkien's *Lord of the Rings*, a place where weary and wounded travelers could find healing and strength to continue their journeys.

Young people were especially attracted to the log build. A haphazard village of tents, trailers, sheds, and one big mobile home formed as a house slowly grew. She told how inexperienced hands learned new skills, created a garden, planted trees, hedges, and a small farm to help feed everyone. Some of the men, including some of Rosemary's sons, found jobs in forestry to support the venture, and she contributed her earnings from her lecture tours in North America and from her books—two big ones due out the following year. Among those attracted to the work and the random community were some with mental-health issues, who found healing and support in the work on the land. Algy also found some peace there, at least for a while. Lothlorien continues to serve people with mental-health diagnoses today, under the guidance of a therapeutic community based on Buddhist principles.

Telling the story about taking risks was gold to people contemplating a similar, very risky decision themselves. Telling her story was also a turning point for Rosemary. She felt welcomed and comfortable in the parish, and she found kindred spirits who shared her vision. In the following months St Ann's became the place she returned to from her lecture engagements, staying at the little house with Marygrace and Nancy, who always kept cheese in the fridge. Whenever she was in Peabody, she joined the study group they hosted.

What she hadn't told the larger group at the retreat was that she faced another major change. Algy had begun drinking again. He had already written a Christmas letter to friends and family saying that the couple had decided to separate but planned to remain friends, which they did. While Rosemary was away, a family friend had visited Lothlorien and reported to her, "I think you need to know something. People really don't want you here." Rosemary was a strong woman and had strong ideas about working hard. Whenever she was at Lothlorien, she spent her days building, planting, milking the cows, making cheese, baking bread, and cooking for the community. When she wasn't at Lothlorien, she was making money to support it. In her absences, other people were growing into leadership roles. Her father also died during this time. It felt like her whole life was changing, whether she liked it or not. On one side of the Atlantic she had found friendship and a new direction, but in Scotland there was uncertainty, rejection, and anxiety about the future and the feelings of her children. It was a hard time for her.

One night before she returned to Lothlorien for Christmas, she went shopping for gifts with Marygrace and Nancy. She suddenly burst out crying and couldn't stop. She had put her heart and soul into the Lothlorien community and had thought she would spend the rest of her life there. But she had reached the decision to leave the community. She felt devastated. "At first I thought I could travel indefinitely and live out of a suitcase," Rosemary remembers. "But I soon realized I needed something more rooted. I needed a new direction, and I felt I'd found one." She knew that she needed this community, this friendship, for her own healing.

On her next visit, Rosemary asked Nancy, "Do you think I could be part of this?"

CHAPTER 2

Loving and Living

Nancy will never forget the day she met Rosemary. Before the retreat, Margaret Kelley, Rosemary's agent, had suggested that some of us from St Ann's set up a time with her to plan it. "Rosemary is coming for a talk at Boston College in a couple weeks," Margaret told us. "Would you like to pick her up at Logan Airport, take her to lunch, then drop her off at her lecture?"

"Yes, of course, we would!" Nancy remembers saying. Many Boston suburbanites go to great lengths to avoid driving to Logan Airport. The group of us women from St Ann's, including Marygrace and Mary Jane, would have done anything to meet Rosemary.

We drove down from Peabody. We were giddy with excitement, for two reasons. We planned to take Rosemary to our favorite Italian restaurant in Boston's North End, Joe Tecce's. On the drive, we chatted about what to order. The cannelloni or the lasagna? And what about a calamari appetizer for the table?

At that time anyone could walk right up to the airport gate, and that's where our group waited for Rosemary to appear. She strode down the jetway in her black boots and a hooded cape she had made herself floating all around her. We were a little in awe of this great woman, Nancy remembers, and I thought she was just gorgeous.

At the restaurant Rosemary opened the menu, immediately closed it, and said, "I'll have the salad. Could you please order for me while I go to the restroom?"

The rest of us looked at one another. She's having the *salad?* We didn't know her at all, Nancy recalls. She was like a saint to us. We felt like, How can we mortals ever measure up? But we stuck to our plan, pasta all around.

The salad, the cape, and the black boots, Rosemary now says, were all bits of the new persona she was constructing—a bit austere, very religious, romantic, and different. It was her refuge from the disintegration of her former life. But the real refuge and her real life was going to be through the group she was meeting that day.

The conversation was warm and lively. I fell in love with her immediately, Nancy remembers. By the end of the retreat, two months later, I knew that I wanted to spend the rest of my life with her. But I was still in my order. And Rosemary was still married.

The differences between us felt as big as the ocean between our homes: Rosemary was middle-class, British, a bit of an introvert, a well-known author and lecturer, self-taught and erudite, opinionated, strong-willed, and a mother of twelve. Nancy was born during the Depression to a working-class union family, grew up as part of a Catholic minority in the American South, entered the convent straight out of high school, and had spent twenty-five years working in the religious schools her order assigned her to. Her kids were her students.

Our friendship quickly deepened over the next year. We told each other our life stories. We had come from different families, educational backgrounds, and career and life choices. But now, well into midlife, we had both landed in the same place—about our faith, worldview, and what we wanted for the rest of our lives. We both were feeling disillusioned. Neither the religious order nor Lothlorien had provided the kind of community we had dreamed of. We were both also exhilarated by the vision that was coming into focus for our group. We discovered the heart of what we shared in common: a fierce desire to create a community based on justice. The fact that we did connect and developed such a deep friendship and love were essential to how Wellspring came about.

***

Rosemary's Story

When I was growing up, Rosemary remembers, our family's lifestyle rose and fell depending on whether my novelist mother, Sylvia Thompson, had spent all the money from her last book before writing the next one. She had started writing and publishing when she was a teenager. Like me, she never got a college degree, though she attended Oxford University, where she met my American-born father, Peter Luling, a linocut artist and wood engraver. When times were good, my sister and I were treated to trips to Europe and to America, where my father lived. We loved that. My mother cowrote a play called "Golden Arrow" with Victor Cunard, which was produced in London's West End starring Laurence Olivier and Greer Garson. Victor's family owned the Cunard shipping line, and he lent us his apartment in a fifteenth-century palace on Venice's Grand Canal. It was a lovely life to dip into. But when the money ran out, or my parents just couldn't cope with us anymore, they sent us to our grandmother Ethel's little seaside house in southeastern England.

My grandmother influenced me more than anyone in my life. She taught me to love history, to value integrity, to regard money as useful but not important, and to show compassion and practicality to the needs she saw. Her Jewish parents had immigrated to Britain from Germany and had started a small chemical business that became the conglomerate International Chemical Industry (ICI). My grandmother's older sisters all "married well" and lived in beautiful country houses. But Ethel's marriage to a Yorkshire man ended because of his infidelity. To be a divorced woman in 1907 was not easy. She was college-educated and earned a little by starting a small school for friends' children. Her sisters helped her out financially, but she hated being dependent. Her sisters were suffragists and gave money to support settlement houses in London that provided housing and services for families who were poor, like Hull House founded by Jane Addams in Chicago. Ethel shared her sisters' concerns, especially for mothers and babies, and took the train into London to volunteer at the settlements. But what she saw there also made her critical of her sisters' luxurious lifestyle.

During World War II we had to move frequently among makeshift homes to avoid bombings. During this time I became a Catholic. I was 16. My childhood sense was that there was a mystery to be found somewhere. In the Catholic churches we had visited in Paris and other cities on our travels, it felt not far away. My parents thought it was "just a phase." Perhaps it was, but it lasted for forty years.

After the war, at age 21, I married Algernon Haughton, another recent Catholic convert. Algy had become a Catholic as an escape from his own family's tightly controlled sect, called the Plymouth Brethren. Born in America, he had dual citizenship and had served in the British Royal Navy during the D-Day landings. When I met him, he was taking an accelerated course for ex-servicemen to become teachers. Very quickly we had six children under age 6, including two sets of twins—leading the one in between to ask, "What happened to my twin?" Six more followed, including two foster children, to make twelve in all.

My career began almost accidentally. My own schooling had been sketchy moving so much as a child, and I never went to college at all. The couple who ran the school in Surrey where Algy got his first teaching job often invited us to dinner to meet their friends. One was Michael de la Bédoyère, an editor who had turned the regional *Catholic Herald* into a challenging, intellectual publication with a national circulation. Based on our dinner conversations, he asked if I'd like to write some reviews, then an essay for a collection in which adherents of various religions or philosophies critiqued their own belief systems. I critiqued Catholicism in a piece called "Freedom and the Individual," denouncing the Church's authoritarianism and calling for freedom of conscience. My opening thesis was, "If the Catholic Church were brought to trial on a charge of restricting the freedom of the human spirit, the counsel for the prosecution would be likely to come into court in a rather more cheerful frame of mind than his opponent." It took a huge amount of research in a local library, but I found I could write it, and I learned an enormous amount.

Reviewers gave my contribution particular praise. That's how my writing career took off. I enjoyed the work, plus I was motivated by the need to augment our family income. I never made much money from books, but the books led to requests for lectures, first in Britain, then in the United States. That did help out financially, both for our family and later for the entire Lothlorien community.

When I first became a Catholic, I imagined "theology" as a set of thick, bound copies on a shelf, like the *Summa Theologica* of Thomas Aquinas. But theology, which comes from the Greek *theos* and *logia,* for god word, is built of words that are in daily use. So they change all the time, incorporating new influences, often unnoticed. The story of Catholic and indeed all Christian theology is a bad-tempered tale, each group convinced its version was the only possible one. Yet words are tricky things, and when we try to use them about God, or god, they are necessarily inadequate and actually deceptive. There are no words for God. The best we can do is to say what God is not, said Meister Eckhart, the great fourteenth-century German theologian and mystic. He was often in trouble with the Inquisition for saying that God is nothing, language now easily recognized in Buddhist spirituality and theology.

What moved people, including me, was not definitions, but stories about people who made a difference, people who changed their own lives, and so changed the world. As a child, I was excited by the lives of saints, who broke the rules, refused to conform, in fact, did things I wouldn't dare to do. Religious words, I discovered, made sense when they were part of a story that moved and changed the hero. The stories in the gospels were about how Jesus's acts and words transformed lives. They gave people new life and a new concept of what life was about.

Much of my own writing was based on stories, both historical and fictional. When I was growing up, homes with children often had Andrew Lang's collections of fairy tales from many cultures. They sparked my imagination and love of telling stories. I later wrote *Tales from Eternity* about how the archetypes and themes of folk tales are central to our own spiritual search: the hero, the evil stepmother, the trickster, and the one that most intrigued me, the girl whom everyone despises or assumes to be helpless but turns out to be the hero, sometimes even disguising herself as a boy to prove she can accomplish what no one else can.

I loved what I called "folk theology." These are the stories from many traditions about nonscriptural incidents. In the Christian tradition, there's a story about Jesus as a child making little birds out of clay and blessing them so they became alive and flew away. In another story, St Bridget is mistakenly consecrated as a female bishop in the fifth century but is also present at the birth of Jesus. Stories of Santa Claus grew around St Nicholas of Myra, a real fourth-century bishop known for his discreet compassion, such as rescuing three girls from prostitution. The greatest number of such stories are about the Mother of Jesus—that she pursued a career independent of her son, as a rescuer, healer, and protector of gay men. Although stories about Mary attract people (and their money), the official Church has regarded them with suspicion.

I thought I was just writing books about what was on my mind and the stories I liked. I didn't realize I was becoming a theologian until somebody at a Dominican retreat house told me I was, and I found I was accepted in those circles. One of my early books actually started a new theological wave of sorts and launched my career as a theologian: *The Transformation of Man: Conversion and Community* (that noun "Man" certainly dates it, something I wish I could change now). It consisted just of stories, incidents from everyday life such as a children's quarrel or a love affair, as well as true stories of the first Benedictine monks and the Separatists who became the American Pilgrims. The stories pointed a way to show how ordinary people can find spiritual self-discovery and live together in community. The book challenged the Church to create those opportunities for spiritual transcendence.

One of my favorite things about those years of writing and lecturing was that I was often the recipient of wonderful hospitality myself. When churches or religious groups invited me to speak, someone in the congregation would frequently offer for me to stay in their home. I accepted whenever I could. Sometimes it was tiring to be a guest on top of traveling and lecturing. But the conversations were always stimulating, and I met so many nice, thoughtful, clever people. I marveled at how in America I could start a tour with New Englanders offering a hand to dig my stuck car out of deep snow, and just days later my Arizona hosts served me grapefruits picked off their tree. I had never seen anything like that.

When I was lecturing in England, I often returned home, if not that night, then in a day or two. The European theologians I was meeting with at that time were primarily interested in Christology and understanding the kind of person Jesus was. But lecturing in the United States, I got a real sense of what everyday people were thinking and wanting to learn about. Many of the faculty I met at universities where I spoke had deep moral objections to the Vietnam War. Some were helping sons and students relocate to Canada or stand firm as conscientious objectors, even some who were veterans themselves. I had already developed the habit of picking up new ideas and pursuing them wherever they led me. In addition to folk theology and Buddhism, I was deeply influenced by the very American movements I discovered when I crossed the Atlantic—fights against the oppression of women, racism, poverty, and the immorality of war—which only got stronger as I got to know Nancy and her commitment to them and as we opened our home to women in poverty. I knew little about feminism or any of these moral struggles before coming to America. As my theology has evolved over my life, one insight has stood out: how much we all still have to learn, and how much we need to constantly learn from one another.

If I'd had a proper theological education, I would never have had those experiences. Plus, I would not have been free to say the things I did, which surely would have been forbidden by Rome. As much as I loved my lecture tours, when I got to St Ann's in Massachusetts, and enjoyed the hospitality of Nancy and Marygrace's little house, I was starting to feel a shift. I had decided I needed to be rooted in a real home and a community.

***

Nancy's Story

Over my lifetime, Nancy recalls, I've seen how lucky I was to be born into a loving family who made sure we had a stable home and a good education and also cared about social justice for others. My parents loved each other, and they loved us three children. In my own career, I've seen how many children don't have that security.

When the United States entered World War II, my feelings of security were disturbed. I was very afraid that my father, a draftsman for a steel company in Allentown, Pennsylvania, would be drafted into the army. No words of assurance could take away my fear. Blackout curtains at night and air raid sirens terrified me. Those sirens haunted my days when I started at St Catharine of Siena School, on the top floors over our church. I was only 5, but I insisted on going to school because my cousin and best friend, Alma, who was 6, was starting. My earliest memories of school are the sirens and all of us shuffling in silence down two flights of stairs to the church, crouching under the pews, head to toe, until the all-clear sounded.

My family's ties to the Pennsylvania steel and coal industry went back generations. My mother's father's family emigrated from Germany to Locust Gap, one of the many small anthracite coal mining towns. My grandfather, "Pappy," started working in the mines at age 14. He was active in the United Mine Workers and had great respect for its president, John L. Lewis, who led the miners to gain living wages, safer working conditions, medical insurance, and a pension program. Lewis's picture hung on my grandparents' kitchen wall alongside a shelf with statues of the Madonna and the Sacred Heart. The adults around me regularly talked about unions, strikes, and workers' rights. I understood when I was very young that these were good things.

During the war my father was recruited to work at Vultee Aircraft, one of the many government-funded manufacturing companies making war planes. Whenever a new plane went for a test flight, he would phone my mother, and we all went outside to look up to the sky to see if we could see it.

When the war ended, my dad helped start a company in the South. The five of us and Joe, our rabbit, rode two long days—no interstates then—to our new home in Asheville, North Carolina. We were the first on both sides of the family to move out of Pennsylvania.

That was the beginning of eight life-changing years. It was the first time we children had seen black people or the impact of Jim Crow laws. White people sat in the front of buses and black people in the far back, if there was room. Water fountains were labeled COLORED and WHITE ONLY. Schools and churches were segregated, and there were "colored sections" in the city.

Catholics were one-third of 1 percent in North Carolina, so it was our first experience of being part of a minority, too. The only Catholic school was St Genevieve-of-the-Pines Academy, which charged tuition. Money in our family was tight. But the sisters were so thrilled to enroll a Catholic family—most of the students were of other faiths—they reduced the tuition. The nuns were informal compared with St Catharine's. Every time I spoke, I stood as I'd been taught and began, "Please, Sister." Finally, my new teacher, Mother Gannon, said, "Child, please relax and sit down. You are making me dizzy with your jumping up and down. You do not need my permission to speak. This is a free country." She smiled, and my classmates clapped. I loved my new school.

In the summer of 1948 my mother, who worked as a nurse, had a radical mastectomy for breast cancer, which left her with little strength in her right arm. My parents hired Inez, an African American woman, to help with housework. The first day, when my mother saw Inez coming, she opened the front door wide and welcomed her in. Inez replied, "Mrs. Schwoyer, please don't ask me to come in the front door. That would not be good for you or me. I will use the cellar door or the back door." I remember holding my mother's hand and thinking, "I want everyone to come in the front door." After she finished work, she'd often sit down with us for a snack before it was time to catch her bus. Sometimes when we took the bus, we'd see her—in the very back seat—and my brother would rush back to sit with her. She gently let us know: "You can't do that. That's where I sit. And I can't go sit up in the seats where you sit." In her years with us, Inez taught us many lessons about what segregation was like for her, as well as about her hopes for civil rights.

Five years after my mother's diagnosis, when I was in high school, she died at our home. In her work as a nurse, she had seen how many nuns had breakdowns, and she really did not want that life for me. Minutes before her death, she opened her eyes and said to me, "I see two of you, and how I wish I had had two of you." So many times during my very full career I thought back fondly on her words and wished that, too. "I love you and want you to do with your life what you want," she went on. "If you want to enter the convent, that's OK."

After graduating, I did just that. My father, sister, and brother drove me up to Milton, Massachusetts, to the novitiate of an order called the Religious of Christian Education, known as RCEs. The order was founded in the nineteenth century after the French Revolution. The Church had been complicit in the monarchy's oppression, and the revolutionaries had abolished all Church institutions, including those that had served people who were poor. Catholic women in France pooled their resources to fill some of the gaps. A group of educated laywomen in Normandy, along with their priest, Abbe Louis Lafosse, formed a religious community with the purpose of providing education for girls, which became the RCEs. Over time they established communities and schools throughout France and Belgium, and later in England, Morocco, Benin, Ireland, and the United States, including North Carolina and Massachusetts.

I loved the community life of the novitiate and the quiet times of prayer and meditation. But I sorely missed my family, all of us still grieving. I made my first vows on August 15, 1956, and happily learned that the RCEs would now study for their bachelor's degrees before teaching in a classroom. The nuns who had gone before us had always been expected to go straight into the classroom after graduating high school, then study for their degrees on weekends and summers. Sometimes it took them ten years.

After college I was assigned to teach biology, advise the newspaper and yearbook, and live on the senior floor for the boarding students back at St Genevieve's in Asheville. Some of the other teachers had taught me when I was in high school. Just three years later, I was asked to be principal of the high school. I was only 25 and not really prepared.

It was a historic time of change: the Bay of Pigs crisis, Vietnam War, Vatican II, the women's movement, civil rights and The March on Washington, then the devastating assassinations of John Kennedy, Martin Luther King Jr, and Robert Kennedy. Our boarding students were from twelve Southern states, and we spent much time discussing and learning about the civil-rights movement, the marches, and racism, such as black-church burnings and police violence using dogs and water hoses.

Most of the women and men who worked for the school—cooks, cleaners, even chauffeurs for the superiors—were black. Some of the workers told us about the extreme poverty in the neighborhood bordering the school on Livingston Street. The faculty and student council asked me to meet with Mr Eddington, the principal of the public Livingston Street Elementary School, to learn if we could "help." Before we sat down to talk, he asked me to walk through the neighborhood with him. I saw homes with dirt floors, minimal or no electricity, and no outdoor space for children to play. Most children had no place to do their homework and no one to help them because parents were working two or more jobs. The school's textbooks were out of date.

I invited him to visit our school and meet the teachers, students, and parents, who in turn visited the Livingston Street School and neighborhood.

That sharing led to imagining an after-school recreation and study program on our campus, with students as tutors and coaches. We called it Project Peace, for the Project for Educational and Cultural Exchange. Four days a week, about thirty St Genevieve's girls walked to Livingston Street and accompanied the children back to our campus for three hours. Half their time was spent tutoring, closely collaborating with the children's teachers at Livingston Street. The other half of their time, the high schoolers coached sports in our gym, swimming pool, and athletic fields—though often the Livingston Street kids had to tell the girls what the rules were. Parent volunteers from Livingston Street and St Genevieve's took turns providing a substantial snack. Many of the St Genevieve's students wrote to us after they graduated to say that Project Peace had been the most important education they had.

My life was full, working with all my heart to get these young Southern women into colleges, traveling for the order, and marching and working for the civil-rights, women's, and peace movements. When news came that Martin Luther King had been killed, I was attending a funeral for the father of the young man who cleaned the school. I was the only white person in the church. Sensing the angry unrest that was about to come, he stood with me and said, "Don't worry. We'll make sure you're OK."

Just two months later, in June 1968, I went to bed like the rest of the world thinking Robert Kennedy had won the California primary and woke up to learn he'd been assassinated. I was shattered. I knew I was close to burnout. I asked for a transfer.

The order assigned me to be a superior to a school and community of sisters in Arlington, Massachusetts, which was a disaster for me and for them. After Vatican II there was tension between those who wanted to keep all the rules, clothes, schedules, and religious life that had been prescribed years before and those who wanted to open to the world. The nuns at my new assignment wanted to be eating supper at five o'clock and watching the news in their pajamas in the community room by seven. The priest actually said to me, "We'll get along fine as long as the car is in the lot by seven." I was champing at the bit to get out to the meetings and the movement work going on in Boston and Cambridge in 1968. I lasted less than a year. What a relief when Marygrace, another RCE, invited me to work with her at St Ann's, and the order agreed.

I was grateful that St Ann's paid for me to get a master's at Boston College in theology and education, where Marygrace had gone. The courses, taught by theologians who embraced Vatican II, combined theology and biblical studies with science, literature, and educational theory to uncover religious meaning in the modern world. Released from the rigid control of the Church, religious education was active, not passive. It was about dialogue and asking questions, not memorizing answers. I was shaped by studying education theorists like Dewey and Montessori, who said we learn through doing. Action in society is key to living the Christian faith.

The exiled Brazilian philosopher Paulo Freire, who was then teaching at Harvard University, as well as at Boston College for summer sessions, was the teacher who influenced me most and affirmed my own experiences as a learner and an educator. Freire rejected what he called "banking education"—the teacher has the knowledge to be learned and deposits it in the minds of the students like depositing money in a bank account. Rather, Freire believed education came through students' experiences. He believed that all persons, no matter how poor or unschooled, no matter how much their voices had been silenced by society, had the ability to look at their own world, think about it, understand it, and take action to change it, through a dialogue with others. Freire's theory not only became the foundation for my future as an educator and activist for social change, but it also helped me to understand and value the first thirty years of my life.

Toward the end of my time at St Ann's, the order asked me to chair an international task force that met in a different country each year to learn how the provinces of sisters were working toward the founding vision of the RCE laywomen who came together to educate girls and women in poverty. Our task was to reform our rules and lives so that we would fulfill that vision. At first, I refused. Already, I was feeling I could do the work of the original sisters better outside the order than in it. I told the superior general that. She said, "We believe that engaging in the process will help you to make your decision. If at the completion of the work, your decision is to leave the order, we will respect that and support you."

By the time we were preparing to found Wellspring, I was in the last year of this work. I had made my decision to leave the order.

***

Our Story

In the months after the two of us met, we spent as much time together as we could, whenever Rosemary was able to stop back in Massachusetts between lecture engagements. Rosemary remembers that she also found herself enormously attracted to Nancy but didn't really know what to do about it. In the summer of 1980 Nancy was in charge of organizing an RCE retreat at the Campion Jesuit Center in Weston and invited Rosemary to lead it. After she had finished her last talk, Rosemary joined Nancy behind the semicircle of eighty nuns, while the provincial superior offered closing words. It happened to be Rosemary's wedding anniversary. She turned to Nancy and said, "I must call Algy." After a bit longer, she took Nancy's hand and whispered, "Do you think we could spend our lives together?"

Nancy couldn't quite believe Rosemary was saying those words aloud. Nancy remembers thinking: Did she just propose to me? I felt scared. And excited. All around were RCE sisters. Over the past decade most of the sisters who had degrees had already left, and many of my friends had married. Of those remaining, only a few knew that I was leaving. One or two sensed our attraction to each other and felt threatened by it. Initially we were careful about letting anyone else know about our relationship. In the 1980s many women didn't talk about loving each other.

Leaving the order was not easy, but I had known for some time I wanted a new and very different life. I knew what I didn't want. I didn't want to live under a hierarchical model anymore. I did not want to be in a traditional parish. I wanted to work for justice. Falling in love at age 40 was wonderful for me and very much tangled up with all those other desires.

Rosemary remembers: Life felt so much simpler on the American side of the Atlantic. Algy and I had already decided to separate, and continuing my lecture tours felt normal and familiar, unlike the turmoil awaiting each time I went back to Scotland. Starting a new venture and a new relationship was an exciting next chapter that felt like a natural next step. When I asked, "Can I be part of this?" I knew that "this" was the community venture, but at the heart of "this" was my deepening friendship with and love for Nancy. Back in Scotland, all my relationships felt more complicated. Most of my children were launched into their own adult lives. The second youngest was 19 and working as an au pair in Italy, and the youngest was studying at a boarding school near where my oldest daughter lived. When she turned 16, we inquired if she could be admitted as a freshman at St Mary's College in Indiana. She spent her breaks with us in Massachusetts. Almost all the now-adult children visited us for periods of time at Wellspring, often with their partners and friends.

Wellspring became the community we both yearned for, a place that would be committed to justice and hospitality, and a home that would enable women to lift themselves up. Who the two of us were, where we came from, and the skills we brought were at the heart of how we lived at Wellspring alongside our guests and how we led the place over three decades.

CHAPTER 3

Finding a Home

That first night of the icebreaking question in our study group at St Ann's, the question that broke everything we thought we knew about our lives, we all agreed: We can't wait two weeks to talk again. Let's meet again next week, and the next, and the next.

What was clear to all of us that night was that we needed to keep talking about our answers to that question: If you could change your life right now, how would you change it?

We needed to pay attention to what those answers had in common. One commonality we saw right away lay in Mary Jane's answer: "I need support. We can't do it alone." Bill, who wanted to leave General Electric but needed the job to provide for his family, needed our support to talk through his options. Rosemary needed to talk about her separation from Lothlorien and Algy and what was next for her. Several of us had the experience of offering hospitality to people in need in our homes and wanted the support of living with others in an intentional community. In one way or another, we all needed support.

After the retreat, and hearing about Lothlorien from Rosemary, some of us started to imagine forming a new community. We thought, if she can do it, we can do it. But none of us wanted to start something new on our own.

We asked ourselves two more questions: Was it possible to do something together? How could we support one another to take the next steps that were practical and spiritually true?

A vision started to materialize. We wanted to practice a kind of hospitality that grew out of our mission for our lives and that addressed the injustices we were seeing in our community: homelessness, poverty, job discrimination, racism, sexism. We didn't know how we would do that.

***

Most of the dreamers in our group had experienced World War II as young adults, as something that directly affected us, emotionally, and as part of our everyday lives, in ways like food scarcity, our friends and family members going to war, and the constant barrage of news of disaster and destruction. World War II was soon followed by the horrors of futile wars in Korea and Vietnam. Our generation now faced the global uncertainty of a nuclear armed world. Yet we also experienced surges of hope, with the creation of the United Nations and the European Union and the liberation of colonized nations in Africa, Asia, and South America. We saw the possibility of rejecting "Power Over" and the hope of creating global systems of "Power With" through genuine democracy.

In the 1960s and 1970s many of us had been part of the civil-rights, peace, and women's movements. It was a time when growing numbers of ordinary people decided to do something about the gross injustice and inhumanity we were seeing, a time of protests and new organizations. Many of us were inspired by the Second Wave of feminism that had broken on the shores of patriarchy, led by women like Betty Friedan. The National Organization of Women created task forces to address women's rights in education, employment, and law, and underpinning everything else, women's poverty.

We were members of a generation that dared to hope for peace and justice, but we were not naïve. The assassinations of John and Robert Kennedy and Martin Luther King Jr were evidence of the deep-rooted forces of resistance to any change that would threaten the forces of "Power Over." For us, the word *justice* was not abstract but a daily presence in the facts of injustice, as the post-war consumerism economy still exploited and left so many behind. For the founders of Wellspring, the struggle against injustice was the reason for undertaking a serious change in how we ourselves lived.

Prior to the 1970s homelessness in the United States had meant men "sleeping rough"—hobos, tramps, bums, winos, mostly single men on park benches and in alleys, roadways, and rail lines. Historically, the numbers of people without homes in the nation, whether they were agricultural migrant workers, people freed from slavery, or people suddenly out of work, had risen and fallen with the economic cycles, often tied to events such as war, recessions, and technological advances such as the railroad and telegraph. When the economy recovered, many of them did, too, and found stable housing.

That changed with the Vietnam War. Saigon fell in 1972, but the war wasn't over. Suddenly a massive wave of returning soldiers, traumatized, drug addicted, and for the first time not welcomed home as heroes, were on the streets. They had not only severe mental and physical wounds but also spiritual wounds. Many found it impossible to reintegrate into a society so sick that it could tolerate the crimes of that war. There was no GI Bill of Rights for them and little public assistance of any kind. Post-traumatic stress syndrome had not yet been recognized, let alone treated.

When Ronald Reagan was elected in 1980 on a mandate to reduce federal funding, he slashed Social Security, Medicaid, food stamps, subsidized housing, mental-health programs, and the anti-poverty Community Development Block Grant program, while expanding the federal deficit with military spending. The 1980s economic growth called Reaganomics benefited only those who were already doing well. Average wages and home ownership fell. Urban poverty and the gap between rich and poor increased. Reagan blamed people who were poor for their poverty—coining the mythical label "welfare queen" as a coded slur for black single mothers. He told a morning talk show that homeless people sleeping on grates for heat did so "by choice." Journalists later tried to find the "welfare queen" that Reagan often referenced and never could, but the myth had been firmly planted in white middle-class consciousness.

Mental-health research at the time was showing that institutionalized patients were harmed by long periods of dependency and separation from their community. Institutions across the country, including the nearby Danvers State Hospital, began discharging patients into "community care," often with no more than $20 in their pockets. But the community-living services envisioned by the advocates of *deinstitutionalization* or *normalization* largely did not exist yet. In practice, people with mental disabilities and mental-health challenges often ended up on the streets.

Banks, real estate agents, and landlords engaged in blatant racial discrimination and redlining, which continues today. Landlords started converting rental properties to condos and told tenants: Here's your notice, or you can buy. Few tenants could. Housing leases and titles were often only in the name of the man in a family. When the police were called for domestic violence, the woman and babies were often expected to move out.

Teenagers increasingly found themselves homeless, something our group of dreamers had direct experience with. Mary Jane and Paul told us stories of pregnant teens they hosted when families kicked the young women out or sent them away to give birth. Two of Rosemary's children first came to her family through the UK foster-care system, at first just for holidays and school vacations, later permanently. From them, she learned how other foster homes treated the children as free household help, harshly punished for any mistakes. When they turned 16, foster children were turned out on their own.

In the 1980s the US homeless population exploded. Estimates ranged anywhere from 250,000 (by the Reagan administration) to 3 million (by the Community for Creative Non-Violence). There was no single cause of homelessness, but many—traumatized veterans, discharged mental-health patients, and the rapidly growing number of people in poverty who lost their homes and could not afford another. Most of the causes were the result of or made worse by federal policies. Homelessness was no longer cyclical but has been a permanent fixture of US society ever since. And the population of people without homes was no longer just single men, but for the first time included many families, women, and children. And most of those families were headed by women.

An inspiration for our vision was Boston's first shelter for men, which had opened in 1969 in a four-story brick building on Pine Street in Chinatown. In the early 1980s, when we started learning about it, the need for beds had outgrown the space—in part due to deinstitutionalization, in part due to the loss of 20,000 lodging-house rooms when the city underwent "urban renewal" and gentrification. Pine Street Inn found a former Boston Fire Department building to shelter 500 men a night. The new inn offered a place to sleep for homeless men and later for women, too, but also clean clothes, clean sheets, medical help, especially for feet, and above all, respect.

Soon afterward Pine Street Inn began to develop permanent affordable lodging houses, with on-site support staff, based on the belief that housing, not shelter, is the answer to homelessness. That belief inspired us as well.

***

As the months went on, we agreed on a few basics: We wanted to share a home with one another and with people who needed a home. That led to two practical questions: Where were we going to do it? And how were we going to pay for it?

Finally, after a year and a half of meeting and talking, in the spring of 1981, Mary Jane said, "We can talk this thing to death. We need to do something."

We began house hunting in April 1981. We needed a house that was large enough for all of us and for the guests we planned to welcome in. We first thought of looking in inner cities, where we knew there was much need. But we also wanted a place of beauty, not only for our own sakes and spiritual health, as the hosts, but also to restore those who came to us in need of help.

That spring Rosemary was visiting. She was anxious to get the project moving. She was hoping the group would find a place before she had to go back to Scotland again right after Easter.

One day Nancy was planning a half-hour trip to Rockport to buy her niece some earrings at a silver shop there. She asked if Rosemary would like to come along and see the former artists' colony out on the tip of Cape Ann, where a red fishing shack known as "Motif Number 1" has been the subject of hundreds of paintings and photographs over the years.

Nancy turned off the highway on to Essex Avenue, to take the scenic route along Gloucester Harbor. In just a couple of miles we passed a large eighteenth-century house, surrounded by high grass that had sprung up with the spring rains, and a big For Sale sign. Nancy made a rapid U turn just before a railroad bridge. We sat outside the house and just stared at it.

"Oh my God," Nancy breathed. "Maybe that's the house."

"I love it," Rosemary said.

Rockport would have to wait. We went straight into Gloucester to look for a real estate agent. We peered in one big window on Main Street and saw that all the employees were men. We couldn't imagine telling them that we didn't actually have any money and we didn't even have a plan, other than we knew we wanted to provide hospitality and shelter for people who needed a home.

We kept walking and found an office with women. One of them greeted us warmly and asked what kind of place we were looking for. We described the house we had glimpsed, and she gave us the details on the listing: First Period house, fully restored with modern additions, on six acres of wooded land. When we told her our intentions, she took a sharp breath in and drew back a little. But she kept listening. "You may want to be more centrally located," she suggested. "Let me find a couple other places you might want to see, too." We made a date.

On April 12, five of us trooped back into Gloucester. We dutifully looked at the three downtown properties the realtor had found. We could barely contain our impatience to show the others the old house that had captivated us at 302 Essex Avenue.

Once inside, we all knew this was the one. The four rooms of the original house were built around a central chimney. One room, with a huge walk-in hearth with a bread oven, had been originally used for both cooking and dining. A sunporch lined the whole width of the house. The original front door with its iron hardware creaked open to a staircase leading up to the second-floor bedrooms. Sometime before World War II, a carport had been added with a large studio above it—room for more bedrooms, we thought to ourselves. Birds fluttered and squirrels ran for cover when we startled them by opening the garage door. We could already imagine a chapel there. We could visualize the porch, kitchen, and common rooms filled with people, safe, sheltered, at home, cooking and eating and learning together. As we walked outside, we could imagine a big garden to grow vegetables and flowers.

Paul ran up the steep hill behind the house and reported that you could see the ocean. Little River ran alongside the property, opening into a tidal estuary across the road that eventually twisted its way out to Gloucester Harbor.

From the first moment the realtor had unlocked the kitchen door, we loved it. It felt hospitable. With very little conversation we had come to a consensus. We now felt an urgency to plan our next move.

We found a diner in Gloucester and sat and talked over bad coffee and very dry brownies. We reviewed the details the agent had given us. Finally Paul said, "We need to make an offer." We went back to the real estate office

Finding a Home

and offered $140,000 of the $145,000 asking price. We signed a purchase and sale agreement that day. When we got back to Peabody, Marygrace rang her lawyer brother, John, and told him the news. Alarmed, he warned, "Don't sign anything else until I see you!"

Paul and Mary Jane had already decided they would sell their home to help buy this one. They wanted to someday leave something to their daughter, Debbie. So they asked our new organization to repay them monthly at a low interest rate—though in the end, they gave us back the interest as a gift. Events moved fast. One day Mary Jane rang Nancy and said, "Sit down. I have a surprise!" Their home had just been put on the market and had sold to the first viewer at the asking price. Not long after, the Religious of Christian Education, of which Nancy and Marygrace were still members, agreed to hold an $80,000 mortgage for the remaining cost. What had been just an idea was now a property with two mortgages.

John McCullough went to work untangling the legal issues—title insurance for a small part of the land with no recorded owner, and a surprise, when it turned out that the sellers owned three acres more than they had realized and agreed to include them without further cost.

John led us through all the legal formalities, including our incorporation as a nonprofit organization in the Commonwealth of Massachusetts. The name almost chose itself. In the front yard stood a well, made of sturdy stone with an iron arch supporting the pulley to draw up buckets of water, fed by a spring. For centuries that well had provided the household with water for drinking, cooking, washing, and gardening. Traditionally, women have met at wells to exchange news, sympathy, and laughs. If you look into this well, you can see the water far down, and if you speak into it, it echoes back, we imagined, with all the voices of those who came before us. Water is life, and Wellspring House was to become a home that enabled and cared for many lives in the coming decades.

***

The house at 302 Essex Avenue was not just a place where the Wellspring story unfolded but a key character in that story. Its history goes back 400 years, with connections to the Salem Witch Trials, a heroic man who earned his freedom from slavery, and tales told by travelers stopping in for a pint at the tavern. The history of the land goes back millennia. When the French explorer Samuel de Champlain first came to Cape Ann in the early 1600s, he encountered the Pawtucket, part of the Algonquian-speaking confederacies of the Northeast. Within a decade, about three-quarters of the native people had died of diseases brought by the Europeans, part of the tragic extinction of indigenous peoples that has occurred worldwide.

One reason European settlers—first the English, and later skilled Portuguese and Sicilian fishing families—came to Cape Ann was the abundance of fish. In 1623 the first English settlers set up a permanent fishing outpost called the Dorchester Company, named after a town in England. The town of Gloucester was formally incorporated in 1642, named after another city in southwest England.

Among the English people first settling on Cape Ann was Sylvester Eveleth from Devonshire in England, who owned a bakery in Boston. He was granted a homestead near Little River, which runs past Wellspring House today, and built a sawmill. The water to turn the wheel came from a reservoir up a steep hill. In the fall, you can wade through golden leaves jeweled with red like a dragon's hoard, past trees whose forbears provided the timber for the European settlers' buildings.

Sylvester Eveleth's son, Joseph, was one of the jurors at the Salem witch trials. The trials were the result of an outbreak of religious hysteria, the horrible fruit of a mixture of fear of anyone different, envy of people who seem wiser, and greed for their goods. One of those who was condemned and hanged, in 1692, was John Proctor. His wife, Elizabeth, was spared because she was pregnant. Joseph Eveleth later signed the Declaration of Regret, admitting that the conviction had been false.

John Davis next bought the property and in 1709 built the house, with its massive beams, wide oak plank floors, and dozens of pegs that locked the framework together. Those pegs—you can see holes where some are missing—stirred Rosemary's memories of building the log house at Lothlorien in Scotland, which used the same methods the Davis family did. Even the children took turns shaping the pegs, sitting astride a shaving horse, as possibly the Davis children did too. The Davises were an enterprising and hard-working family. In a society where everyone drank beer, one of the businesses they undertook was also a place of hospitality, a tavern.

The most remarkable story connected to the house is that of Robin Freeman, who was enslaved by a sea captain named Charles Byles, who lived across the road from the house. In 1769 Robin was able to buy his freedom by paying Captain Byles one pound and twelve shillings. Robin then left to farm rented property in the Magnolia neighborhood of Gloucester. We wish we knew more about how Robin lived as a free black man for more than a decade. Slavery did not end in Massachusetts until 1783.

Robin's only child, Robert, became the largest landowner in Magnolia, and his grandson became Salem's first black police officer. In 1826 Robert bought the house now at 302 Essex Avenue. To make ends meet, the family rented out the southern two rooms, one downstairs and one up, divided at the staircase, and later sold that half of the house. Freeman family members lived in the house until the last of them, Robin's great-granddaughter, Hattie Freeman Johnson, died in 1931. In old age Hattie granted ownership of her two northern rooms to Henry and Margaret Oakes, with this provision: that she could continue there as long as she was well enough, an agreement that has echoes in our story almost a century later.

In 1932 the rooms of the house were reunited under one owner, when the Keffer family acquired both halves on the same day. They also built on a six-room two-story addition. The house again became a place of hospitality, when the Keffers opened a tearoom under the sign "Stage Coach Inn" and dated it 1649. However, the house was not built until sixty years after that, it was never an inn, and it couldn't have been a stagecoach stop, given that it's within walking distance of Gloucester. But it was a nice idea.

We happily got to know one of the next families who lived in the house. Once we had settled in, Winnie and Dick Bell, who had raised six children there, stopped by to welcome us. Dick had laid the brick floors in the two-story addition, including a second staircase, which features prominently in the end of our time in the house. A great many Bells became part of our story—serving on our board, donating design services, and opening their home for our fund-raising events.

When we first saw the house, the residents were three men and three Persian cats. The smell of cats was colossal. Not until after our first Thanksgiving, with all the aromas of baking and roasting, did we finally obliterate that smell. The sink, toilet, and shower in the downstairs bathroom are still a very masculine black ceramic. On a later visit, we brought our former RCE Provincial Superior, Mother Sharry, to see the house. One of the owners emerged from that bathroom with nothing on but a towel. Without missing a beat, she said, "Thank you so much for selling us this house."

***

In the days before we could move into our new home, the founders had some intensive talks about how we planned to live together and make decisions as a community. We agreed on several principles to govern our shared life. Each of us would pay our way as individuals and were responsible for personal expenses, such as our cars and insurance. Each of us would contribute $500 a month, as we could, to a common annual budget of $30,000, to cover the mortgage and household expenses. Anyone who decided to leave the community could not have any claims against the organization. Another decision was to pay property taxes to the city, although as a nonprofit organization, we could apply for exemption, as most nonprofits do. We wanted to make clear from the start that we would be part of the local community and wanted to contribute to our share of local services such as streets, schools, library, and fire and police services. We also agreed to shop locally in order to support the local economy.

While we completed the legal and practical preparations, the previous owners allowed Mary Jane and Paul to move some of their furniture into the house, which we were grateful for. Most of us didn't have any furniture of our own. They placed a statue of the Madonna that had belonged to Paul's mother in a flower bed in the front of the house.

The closing took place on August 3, 1981, with Mary Jane and Carol Provenzano representing Wellspring. It was fitting that Carol was there. She and Dick completely supported our venture. After their daughter Mary died, her presence remained with her family, and they knew they could ask her help about important things. Dick told us, "I don't pray to her for just anything, but this matters." When we first told Carol the location of the house we had found, she said, "I think that's the house my grandmother lived in." She checked with her mother, who said that Mary's great-grandmother had been a tenant in the house. She met her husband when he was working on the railway bridge that connected Gloucester to Boston, only 100 yards from the house. Mary's picture always had a place of honor in our living room.

***

We cannot overstate how essential Mary Jane and Paul Veronese were to making Wellspring House possible. They were the only ones among us who owned their home, a key financial asset they allowed us to make use of. Paul was the only one who had a salaried job with benefits, which he gave up, even though he had recently completed his doctorate in education.

Both of them deeply valued education, not just formal education but also an intense desire for knowledge. After graduating from Peabody High School, Paul enlisted in the Navy, served on submarines in the Pacific, and used the GI Bill to get his bachelor's degree at Merrimack College while working full-time for the post office. He started teaching English at the high school and rose eventually to assistant superintendent. He was devoted to every part of his job, big and small. Paul was the one who called snow days and sometimes was out snow blowing himself to make sure the sidewalks were safe for the children going to school. He also took on a major project developing early childhood education in Peabody's public schools. And he was in charge of the federal Title I after-school and vacation programs for income-limited families in the North Shore region, including Gloucester. Paul loved children and wanted all children to have equal education opportunities.

Mary Jane had worked at General Electric during the war years until their daughter Debbie was born. It was very important for her to be a full-time mother. Once Debbie was grown, Mary Jane worked as coordinator of the middle school religious education program at St Ann's. For her, the Wellspring experience had begun fourteen years earlier, when she traveled to South America. "I became aware of what poverty meant," she told us later, "of a lifestyle so different that encountering it was a kind of conversion. My family was not well off, but just not having things you really needed was something I hadn't ever imagined. And later, when I went to Haiti, that really changed me. I wanted to make some contribution. But I knew I couldn't live in Haiti—too many bugs!"

After Debbie went to college, Paul and Mary Jane started taking in pregnant young women, one at a time, through an organization called Birthright. The young women were often just teenagers, whose families wanted them out of sight until the baby could be put up for adoption. They were truly in crisis, their bodies undergoing enormous physical and hormonal transformation, cut off from all the relationships in their lives. With Birthright's help, Mary Jane and Paul provided emotional support, maternity clothes, and helped with reconciliation with their families. The work was fulfilling, but there was no respite. Their guests were still so young, and the two of them could never get away for a vacation, weekend, or even out for the evening, depending on the situation. "It became very exhausting," Mary Jane told us. "You need other people to sustain it."

Paul said more than once that as Mary Jane had supported him through his college years and career, he in his turn would support her desire to live in the kind of mission-based community that we were all now envisioning. Paul was always very deliberate in his approach, weighing all aspects, but when he made up his mind, his commitment was solid. Without the two of them, not just their financial help but all the skills they brought, Wellspring could not have been founded.

***

By the time we moved in, two more women had joined our founding group. Jenny Richards had entered the Religious of Christian Education order right after high school graduation, just as Marygrace and Nancy had. Jenny had taught at and soon become principal of a Catholic elementary school in Hendersonville, North Carolina, much as Nancy had in Asheville, just ten miles away. Jenny loved the religious and class diversity of her students, and she loved living near the Smoky Mountains. She would have been happy to live there for the rest of her life, she often said. But her elderly mother in Massachusetts was in poor health, and Jenny wanted to spend whatever time her mother had left, helping with what she needed or wanted. Jenny also wanted to live in a community committed to social justice. When she heard about Marygrace and Nancy's plans for Wellspring, she asked if she could be part of it. We all said yes.

On a frigid night the previous February, a teenager named Kathleen LaVoie, whom everyone called Sissy, rang Marygrace and Nancy's doorbell. Nancy opened the door, and Sissy nearly collapsed inside. Nancy knew the first priority was to get Sissy a hot tub and a warm bed. She then rang the police to let them know where Sissy was and that she was safe.

Sissy was in the same grade as Mary Provenzano at school. She had started coming to St Ann's religious education classes when she was 7 or 8 years old and was later a leader in the youth group, one of the only places where she could have fun with friends. Her mother drank, and there was always a series of men in the house, some of whom beat Sissy's mother and terribly abused her three children. The children often had nothing to eat. Sometimes the police called Father Moritz, who always asked Marygrace or Nancy to accompany him to the house.

The February night that Sissy walked out of her childhood home, she knew that if she stayed, she would die. She didn't even know how she ended up at Nancy and Marygrace's front door. In the days to come, Marygrace contacted Sissy's aunt and uncles to ask if she could live with them until she finished high school in June. They all said no. They didn't want to get involved.

Nancy gave up her bedroom and slept on a fold-out loveseat in the living room to give Sissy some privacy. "I knew this was a huge sacrifice," Sissy remembers, "but she never once made me feel guilty or unwanted in any way. Even when I didn't feel worthy, they always showed me that I was worthy, simply by listening to me, believing me, showing me respect, and making me feel that I mattered."

Nancy and Marygrace accompanied Sissy the day she became an emancipated minor and again the day she took her mother and stepfather to court, filing a Section 51A report of abuse or neglect. That helped ensure her younger sisters and brother would be fed and attend school, and all four of them would have to attend weekly group therapy. Nancy, Marygrace, and Rosemary were also by her side at her graduation to receive her adult high school diploma, after working so hard at a full-time job by day and studying at night. "It felt wonderful knowing they were proud of me, which is something I never experienced before," Sissy said.

Once the group found the house, Nancy and Marygrace knew they'd be moving. They agreed: Their home was Sissy's home. They asked if she'd like to come live with them and the others and be part of the new venture in hospitality and social justice. "Absolutely," Sissy said. But she added emphatically, "Not as a kid. I want to work and be part of it."

Now we were seven: Paul and Mary Jane Veronese, Marygrace McCullough, Nancy Schwoyer, Rosemary Haughton, Jenny Richards, and Sissy LaVoie.

We all had to find part-time paid work for our $500 monthly contribution. In order to devote more time to Wellspring House, Paul left his school administration position and got a job with the post office again. Mary Jane found work, first as a waitress and later as a secretary. Nancy got a job supervising adult education for the Archdiocese of Boston. Rosemary was still earning fees by lecturing around the country. Marygrace had just finished her doctorate in pastoral counseling and had started seeing clients. Jenny taught as a substitute in the Gloucester elementary schools. Sissy was studying at the University of Massachusetts in Lowell and working part-time for Head Start and got holiday retail jobs.

Working to pay for our mortgage and expenses together this way certainly made 302 Essex Street feel like our home. But more deeply, in the months to come, we would make it ours by the ordinary things we did together. The smell of Rosemary's new bread and of Jenny's cookies—she had to hide them from Paul—and the sight of fresh-cut flowers and colorful garden vegetables, soon told visitors that this was indeed home. After Paul cut the grass, which had been knee-high, our new neighbors warmed to us in our home too.

Our next job was to turn our vision of inviting guests to stay with us into a reality. Homemaking was the ground on which the whole mission of social justice would grow, in a space fit for human beings. Our idea of hospitality was not choosing to have friends over, but a moral imperative, a work of justice, responding to our outrage at a system that regarded poverty and homelessness as acceptable. Wellspring House was the place where we would practice radical hospitality.

***

Finding a Home

As a prelude to the moving day, a team of friends from St Ann's parish descended on the house with brooms, mops, and buckets. On the day of the move there was a final picnic lunch in Mary Jane and Paul's empty house for the volunteer movers and the many friends from Peabody who had been supporting the whole project.

We wanted all our friends and supporters to understand what we and they were getting into, so shortly after we moved in, we wrote them a letter. Reading it now, we can see the shape of the new community and our ideals, but we could not guess how it would grow. We described ourselves as "*a group of Christian people ... who have bought a house in which they will live in community ... [O]ne part of its purpose is to be a place of hospitality for people in trouble, for instance, abused women and children and homeless young people ... [T]hey might need to come for a short time until more permanent solutions could be found ... or in some cases for longer periods ... [T]he aim of the community and the house is to create a lifestyle and an atmosphere which is hospitable, simple and open and adaptable to new people, new ideas and new needs, so that the way we live there together ... may be an expression of the possibility that there is a realistic alternative to competition, waste, and exaggerated individualism; that human beings can share their lives in such a way as to liberate the individual while being sensitive to the human and ecological community that is creation.*"

This home was never intended to be just for us. We knew we would need to make alterations to the house, renovating spaces to create more bedrooms and a place for quiet, ritual, and meetings. The work was paid for with a personal loan from Paul.

Shortly after we started the renovations, the Gloucester building inspector, Hank Camille, showed up at the house asking to see our building permit. We didn't have one, as our contractor had not obtained one. Mr Camille asked us a lot of questions about who we were and what we were doing. As we talked, we realized that a recent lawsuit the Unification Church had brought against the City of Gloucester had made him—and likely other people in the small city—suspicious about another group of unrelated adults moving there to do "good work."

For the past few years local and national papers had run stories about how the Moonies, as the followers of the Rev. Sun Myung Moon were called by outsiders, had used an intermediary buyer to purchase a thirty-room waterfront

Tudor mansion, which had been given to the Catholic Church by a town patriarch. They also bought a seafood processing plant and a popular local restaurant with docking privileges. The working-class townspeople felt invaded. Some feared the church would lure young people into a cult. But the biggest fear was that the Unification Church, with its massive stores of capital and low-cost labor from members, would get control of Gloucester's lifeblood, the fishing industry. A figure of Moon was hanged in effigy in the harbor. The City Council passed an angry resolution comparing the Unification Church to Jim Jones and his suicide cult, which was later rescinded on advice of the city attorney. Mayor Leo Alper fought the church's expansion for most of his eight years in office. When the city told the church it had to apply for a change-of-use permit and adapt the mansion to meet a building code, the cRhurch sued, asserting it was not changing the religious use of the mansion. It also charged the city with violating its members' civil rights. On his last day in office, the mayor signed an agreement with the church, regulating the property, setting payment for municipal services, and settled the lawsuit. Living fifteen miles away in Peabody, we hadn't paid that much attention to the stories or thought about how they would affect Gloucester people's views of us.

"Why don't you go somewhere else?" was the inspector's plaintive question. He told us we could go to City Hall and get a building permit for the new addition we were building, but he would never approve an occupancy permit for so many unrelated people living together. We appealed, a process that took several months.

That interaction got us thinking more, generally, about how we presented ourselves to our neighbors and anyone we met in town, including the workers we asked to help us. Among ourselves, we had taken for granted that all of us would share in the planning and decision making, although we had different roles. When workers had questions about the work, they would ask for "the boss." They meant Paul, the only male in the house. Nancy would always reply, "I can help you." Some had a hard time accepting that there was no boss and that a woman could give them the information or orders they needed. It was one of the important points when we had to express out loud the principles of our common venture. Later, we called it *mutuality*.

CHAPTER 4

Homemaking

On December 8, 1981, our mission of hospitality took the form of a real young woman, Ellen Kelly. The local Red Cross director had seen a newspaper story about our appeal over the denial of our occupancy permit and been among the first to show up at our door to introduce himself and find out what we were doing. Not long after, Red Cross staff brought Ellen, traumatized, carrying just two bags of donated clothes, to our door.

She had been rescued on Thanksgiving Day from a burning house, where she lived in return for fetching beer and cigarettes for a bedridden old man. He had dropped a cigarette in his bed and set it on fire. Ellen had tried to get him out through a window, but he was too heavy. He died in the fire.

Gradually, we learned the story of her life. Born to a single mother, she had been cared for by elderly foster parents since birth. She in turn cared for them as they got older. When they died, their daughter told her she had to go. For years, she had couch surfed, made money however she could, and often spent it playing bingo, which she loved. Now 29, she had no money and no home.

Our second guest came that same afternoon. Sissy called us from the hospital. Her 16-year-old sister Heidi needed refuge from the continuing abuse in her home. Her mother's boyfriend had kicked her black and blue and given her three broken ribs after she asked for a paper bag to put her things in.

We were still renovating the rooms over the carport, which didn't yet have heat, electricity, or plumbing, and we were still waiting for the occupancy permit for the new construction there. So we lodged our two guests in the bedrooms of the original early-eighteenth-century house. The two of us slept in the unfinished new rooms. Rosemary heated a couple of bricks on the woodstove and wrapped them in towels for the foot of the bed.

In February, our third guest, Marian, came with her 4-year-old son. She had recently been diagnosed with multiple sclerosis, and her husband had left her and their son rather than be burdened with a sick wife.

Suddenly, *hospitality* was not just a word but a daily way of life. Each of the people who came to us had their own needs, personalities, and life stories, as well as skills and hopes. They required not only beds and food but also friendship and support to take the next steps in their lives, especially finding homes. We got busy introducing ourselves to local ministers and anti-poverty, welfare, employment, and housing organizations that had resources that could help our guests. Many of those local service providers became friends and supporters for decades. People in town started to learn what we were doing and wanted to help.

We had already incorporated as a nonprofit organization in Massachusetts, but we also needed to gain charitable status, so donors could claim tax deductions. That would also exempt Wellspring House from paying tax on goods. The Internal Revenue Service denied our first application on the grounds that community members were benefiting financially by living in the house. John McCullough advised us to find a local lawyer. We hired Rick Porter, who was a City Council member, who seemed to fall a little in love with us. On his advice, we applied again, designating $350 of our $500 individual monthly contributions to the house as rent and $150 as donation. The application was approved.

***

The next application to deal with was our occupancy permit. In February 1982 the City Council heard our appeal at City Hall, with its vast 1930s murals funded by the Works Progress Administration. We discovered the council chamber filled with about 100 people, our board members, local clergy, representatives from various agencies, and friends we had made in the six months we had lived and worked in Gloucester. Rick Porter explained our appeal, and the council members asked a few questions. Then they invited members of the community to ask questions or make comments. One after another, we heard support and enthusiasm. Several people had also sent letters of support.

Finally the chair asked if anyone wanted to speak against our application. There was only one, a neighbor rose to say that he had come there to object. He was thinking about the old stigma of alcoholic single men. But after hearing all the positive words, he felt like a lion that had lost its roar. The council granted us an occupancy permit as a licensed lodging house, the only category that allowed unrelated people to share a house. The hall broke into such applause and cheering that the chair had to raise his voice to ask the celebration to continue elsewhere so the council could get on with its work. We went back to 302 Essex Avenue and popped open some champagne.

By the time we got the permit, we were not only welcoming guests, but it was time to plant our garden. We believed that caring for people also meant caring for the land. Later we spelled out in our mission statement: "Every life touches every other life." All creatures live by the hospitality of the earth, which depends on our care of it. From the start an organic garden was part of the plan.

Rosemary had been puzzled to hear her American friends talk of "putting in a garden." In England, a house's whole lot, large or small, was called the garden, where one could have a lawn, a vegetable garden, flower beds, or all of those. For more than thirty-five years Rosemary cultivated Wellspring's garden, growing both vegetables and flowers throughout the property. She was thrilled to have a much longer growing season in Massachusetts than in Scotland. Like any true gardener, she always hankered to get out in the dirt as soon as the ground thawed, even though hard-core New Englanders warned her over and over that the last frost could come right up to Memorial Day.

From March through October, Rosemary was in the garden at six every morning, often accompanied by volunteers, such as Steve Carter, who later joined our staff. Steve loved to display the greens, eggplants, cauliflowers, and carrots in a wide basket for everyone to admire in all their colors, just as Rosemary constantly arranged vases of daffodils, tulips, lilies, mums, and asters, their pops of color all through the house throughout the growing season. Volunteers and guests helped pick black currants, strawberries, and other fruit for jams that lined the pantry shelves. We and our guests feasted on their beauty, with our eyes, noses, and tastebuds. Often local nurseries gave us plants and even trees at the end of the season for fall planting. Many are still growing. New shelter guests were sometimes surprised to see Rosemary—who more often wore long skirts—out in blue jeans, a large denim shirt, a bandana on her head, and wellies brought back from England on her feet. Everything the garden produced, lovingly displayed, became a signature of the house, letting visitors know that this was a true home, and they were welcomed with true hospitality.

***

Looking back, we find it hard to comprehend just how much we accomplished in the first two years, each new challenge helping develop our own understanding of our mission. The view in retrospect is like a speeded-up film of a tulip opening, as the opening petals reveal more streaks of color unfolding from the hidden heart and spreading themselves to the sun. As in all nature, there were darker colors, too—the stories of grief, pain, and loss our guests brought with them—as well the bright times of joy and fulfillment.

The new rooms were now fully occupied by guests. Some just turned up. Some were referred to us. At first the only criteria for guests that we had agreed on was that we could not accept people with addictions unless they were in a recovery program nor people who needed nursing care. We didn't have the skills or conditions to help them and protect others in the house.

Each of those who came to us had their own stories, often heartrending ones. A local pastor brought a teenage boy to us. He had been turned out of his home because his parents said he had sexually abused his sister. While with us, he was able to graduate from Gloucester High School. Some of us went to his graduation ceremony and hosted a party for him afterward. We also helped him find a home, in a house we later started for single men. Eventually it became clear that the accusation had been false. Another relative had been the abuser, but the young man never returned to his family. When he moved out of Wellspring House, he gave us a wrought-iron pot with a pan holder that he had made in the high school metal workshop. Occasionally we bumped our heads on the low-hanging frying pan. But we cherished his gift, which hung in the Wellspring kitchen for more than twenty-five years. Sadly, he lost his eyesight, his general health deteriorated, and he died while still in his 20s.

Another memorable guest was an elderly woman who had been in an abusive marriage, enduring it out of respect for her marriage vows and pressure from her pastor to accept the abuse as "the will of God." She saw a story about Wellspring in the local newspaper and cut it out. Her husband allowed her to leave the house only to go to church or a prayer group. One morning she showed up at Wellspring with nothing but her Bible. Eventually she filed for divorce and got permission from the court to remove her half of the home's furnishings. Several Wellspring community members, accompanied by two policemen, went with her. In time she recovered not only her health and her possessions, but she found her voice to express her strong opinions. She did not always approve of the way Wellspring was run. We used cloth napkins, but she thought we needed napkin rings, too. We tried them, but they were too fiddly for us and our guests. She also did not think our younger guests got enough corrections in their manners and were not grateful enough for our hospitality. She took it on herself to bark "Thank you!" or "Please!" whenever they were speaking, to remind them.

An elderly man came to us after his home burned down and his wife had died in the fire. He was in shock and deep grief, but he was also anxious to go back to the site to look for commemorative plates he had bought though advertising flyers. He was convinced the plates were valuable and would make him rich enough to buy a new house. With permission from the fire department, Paul went with him to search, but there were only a few bits, no intact plates. After a few months at Wellspring he got housing in one of Gloucester's senior housing projects, and volunteers collected furnishings for his new home.

A young woman showed up fleeing an abusive boyfriend. Her brother came to the house and demanded that she come home. "It's all lies," he yelled. "I can't see any broken bones!" She stayed, but we realized that we were too publicly known to be a safe place for women fleeing abuse. We got to know some safe houses in private homes to which we could refer abused women and families. At the same time a support group formed and became Help for Abused Women and their Children (called HAWC), which later opened a shelter whose address was not public.

The two of us had studied women thinkers of our time and called ourselves feminists. We had spent the first half of our lives pushing the boundaries of what women could be and could do, in the Church and schools, in Rosemary's lectures and books, and in Nancy's work in the women's movement. But when we started welcoming women who were poor into our home and saw what they were up against, we realized how very much we still had to learn. Over and over we had to learn that lesson.

Soon after we started welcoming guests, an abused teenager who had been staying with us suddenly just disappeared. We were worried sick. She was so young and so troubled. Two days later she showed up again, looking terrible. Her face was pale. She came in and collapsed on the floor. We were relieved to have her back but worried about how she was, where she'd been, and what had happened. "You want to know where I was?" she cried out. "OK, so I'll tell you. I had an abortion!" We may have thought we had worked through our ideas on abortion, reconciling the positions of the Church, medical scientists, and women's movement leaders. But nothing had prepared us for the emotion that surged over us, when we were confronted with a 17-year-old in our home who was so alone in the world, who didn't know what to do, and this is what she had to do. We had women coming to us beaten up, women struggling to be good parents, making the best choices they could. It radicalized us so fast. Each time we saw more clearly how every part of our society, including institutions we were part of, objectified and devalued women. As Rosemary wrote in *Song in a Strange Land*, "There is a sense in which all women, with a few exceptions, are 'homeless,' even if they live in comfortable homes, because they belong to the sex that does not possess, that is, on the contrary, possessed."

***

In fall 1982 we welcomed a new resident community member, Mark Baker, an Episcopal priest looking for experience beyond parish work. Mark had read some of Rosemary's books, and he sought the two of us out after a liturgy at the Paulist Center in Boston. Mark had been active in Bread and Roses, a soup kitchen founded in 1980 in the nearby city of Lawrence.

He was also a trained musician with a lovely voice and could play several instruments. Paul was grateful to have another man in the house. Living with six women, he had always been a terrific sport and learner, gamely going along with the community's agreements, such as hanging his own clothes on the line, hauling out the ironing board on Sunday nights, and packing his own suitcase, all the things Mary Jane had done for him in their previous home.

In addition to bringing more music into the house, Mark brought us candy, really exquisite stuff. To pay his share of the expenses, he took a job with a high-end maker of chocolates with a nautical theme called Harbor Sweets in nearby Marblehead. The owner had surveyed chocolate makers for their ideal piece of candy. He came up with sailboat-shaped Sweet Sloops, a triangular almond toffee buttercrunch, dipped in dark chocolate for the boat, white chocolate for the sails, and crushed almonds for spindrift. Corporations gave them as fancy gifts to clients, and wedding planners often bought them as party favors. Mark often brought home some of the less-than-perfect specimens, which tasted just as good as their aristocratic companions.

We all knew that taking regular times for sharing and reflection was essential amid the demanding routines of daily life. Our whole motivation was spiritual. We wanted to explicitly welcome all faiths, but we hadn't yet figured out how to create an ecumenical worship experience at Wellspring. Mark's arrival motivated us.

The original group was all Catholic, and we had started out thinking we would attend daily Mass at local parishes. That didn't last long. We were so spoiled by worship at St Ann's, with a liturgy committee that made sure worship services moved and spoke to us, as well as a professional organist, a fantastic choir, and a folk group Marygrace had started. The local churches followed the rules, but they hadn't caught up with Vatican II and the sense of God being within and among us that Rosemary wrote and lectured about. There was rarely congregational singing, usually just a screechy organ and sometimes a soloist.

We also tried the informal afternoon Masses at the Jesuit retreat house out on Eastern Point, scenically overlooking the ocean. One afternoon, a Wellspring volunteer and guest, Richard Kontos, took a walk on the retreat center grounds. A talented carpenter and a conscientious objector who refused to pay taxes that supported weapons of war, Richard was at a low point in his life. The IRS had caught up with him and confiscated his tools from his car. He was suffering from depression and was staying with us for a few months. One of the Jesuits stopped him and said he couldn't walk there if he wasn't a retreatant. Nancy called to express her disappointment at their lack of hospitality. We didn't go back.

Richard made us a low table for our newly created chapel in the former garage, a simple square space that we completed with some chairs and cushions. There, we lit candles and read scripture passages and other sources that inspired us in our mission. After Mark joined us, we had live music. We had been using a very simple Eucharistic ritual—bread that Rosemary made and wine to commemorate Jesus's Last Supper and our connections as one spiritual body—drawing on a book of rituals created by Anglican St Hilda's community members who were exasperated by sexism in the church, called *The New Women Included*. When Mark, an ordained Episcopal priest, arrived, Jenny suggested he lead our liturgy. Mark said a very firm "No!" He didn't feel right in that role. So we started taking turns preparing and leading a homemade liturgy during our weekly reflection time. Sometimes our guests and friends joined.

A rhythm started to establish itself in our daily life. It was shaped by the ongoing practical needs, emotional and physical, of the resident community members and our guests, as they interacted with one another and with volunteers, neighbors, friends, and donors. The two of us had stayed at a couple of Catholic Worker houses, where we tried to overlook the fact that the sheets where we slept hadn't been changed all that recently. We deeply respected the work and philosophy of Dorothy Day and the Catholic Worker Communities, welcoming anyone unconditionally. But we believed that respect for our guests included not just serving them, but also expecting them to share in the work that made hospitality possible. All of us living at Wellspring House—residents and guests—took turns with cooking, doing the dishes, and cleaning.

Breakfast was self-serve because of differing job and school schedules. But everyone who was in the house at lunch or suppertime ate meals we prepared together on the big sunporch. The first year we managed to celebrate

Thanksgiving there with the help of electric heaters. In winter we had to crowd into the dining room, where there was a small woodstove. In fall 1982 we installed a woodstove on the sunporch so we could eat watching the seasons turn, close to the outdoors. Fetching wood, tending the fire, and clearing the ash became part of the ritual of daily life.

Before supper everyone gathered and gave thanks for the food, for those who had grown it, and those who had cooked it. The children loved to give thanks. This ritual of eating together was new for some of our guests. Some protested, but most came to enjoy it. Several parents cautioned us that their children did not like vegetables, except for things like baked beans or canned corn. More often than not, when the children saw other people eating broccoli, carrots, cucumbers, peppers, or cabbage from the garden, they wanted some too. A mother worried about wasting food might say to a child taking a big helping of broccoli, "You're not going to eat that." Mary Jane would always say, "Why don't you let them try some?" Even the mothers couldn't get over how good the garden vegetables tasted. Sometimes after they got established in their own homes, we would run into them in the grocery and they'd tease us, "Thanks to you, I have to buy fresh vegetables!"

Guests could keep their own rooms as they wanted, but once a week they had to change their sheets and take a mop upstairs. On Saturdays all of us shared in cleaning the house for about an hour and a half—dusting, polishing, vacuuming, washing floors. Some resisted a little, but the chore schedule rotated so there could be no argument about fairness. "I loved this day because there were lots of jokes, some music, and laughter," Sissy remembers. "In the end the guests had a sense of accomplishment, of being part of a community. They felt good for contributing, and the rest of the day was theirs."

Every Thursday the community met to discuss house issues, guests' progress, and new guests who were arriving and how we could prepare to help them. Board meetings were once a month on Sunday evenings by the fireplace in our living room. We started to invite local leaders to join our board and were grateful that so many said yes: social workers, teachers, an attorney, a vice-president of a local bank, a city councilor, and representatives of local agencies, such as the Red Cross and Action Inc, the anti-poverty agency of Cape Ann. Two outsiders also joined and contributed their experience: Edwina Gateley, originally from England, was leading ground-breaking work in Chicago with women sex workers; and Father Frank Kelley, one of the founders of the Pine Street Inn in Boston.

Unlike some social workers, Frank did not label homeless individuals and families as dysfunctional. He knew from his experience at Pine Street and his parish that once homeless people had a home, they often no longer needed therapy and other intervention. Frank's mother was Margaret Kelley, Rosemary's lecture agent who had become a dear friend of Wellspring. We visited her at her home in Sandwich, Massachusetts, on Cape Cod. Margaret hated waste. She kept her potatoes and onions in the clothes dryer to make sure she didn't use that energy-sucking appliance. We also enjoyed listening to her stories of being on the campaign trail for the Kennedys. She described one plane ride in a thunderstorm. Most people onboard were sitting white-knuckled. But Rose, mother of Jack and Bobby and seven other Kennedys, placidly prayed her rosary beads.

"I loved those times," Sissy says, "and I loved being a founder and one of the staff. At the community meetings we would relax and touch base and share a little of ourselves and what was going on or coming up in our personal lives."

***

In the spring of 1982 two women came into our lives who cherished the same sense of mission as we did. This couple mirrored our own views, histories, and desires for our personal lives, and we quickly became fast and lifelong friends. Over the years we inspired and challenged one another in ways that helped us better articulate and accomplish each of our life's work. Ann Louise Gilligan was from Ireland, and Katherine Zappone was from Seattle. Both were in their first year of their doctoral studies in theology at Boston College. They had met each other at the beginning of that academic year and immediately fallen in love. To have private space to be together, they spent weekends in Gloucester.

Rosemary's book called *The Catholic Thing* had just come out, and Ann Louise and Katherine had seen a poster for her talk at the college that spring. Toward the end of her talk, Rosemary had mentioned Wellspring

House, where she was living with a group in Gloucester who had made a common commitment to social justice by offering hospitality to those who needed it. Ann Louise and Katherine were so taken with what they heard, they came up afterward and introduced themselves.

The next Sunday they were eating breakfast at Charlie's Place, a popular restaurant in Gloucester, and decided to see if they could find Wellspring House. They asked three policemen at a nearby table if they had heard of the house. "Just your luck," one of them said. He had read an article about the house in the *Gloucester Times* the week before and gave them directions. They enthusiastically jumped in their car.

About fifteen minutes later they pulled into our driveway and knocked on the door. Nancy answered and invited them in for a pot of tea. We talked for hours that very first spontaneous afternoon together. We told them about our group of good friends who had decided to radically change our lives and how we had given up our homes and jobs to live together and welcome those who had no home.

We heard about their studies and stories, too. They later found a house to rent in nearby Beverly Farms, and we spent many wonderful hours sharing meals and talking on their screen porch. Ann Louise had an idea about how imagination is central to transformation, whether personal or societal, which became her dissertation. Whatever you can imagine, you can do. You have to see it, smell it, and keep imagining it as it changes. That idea was at the heart of our experience as well. Their ideas and work continued to shape us as Wellspring grew and changed over the decades.

We also influenced the two of them. After they completed their studies, they founded an educational center called The Shanty in the hills outside Dublin, Ireland, to help low-income women get off welfare. As at Wellspring House, a foundational principle was to first listen to the women's stories to discover what they wanted and what was needed to make that possible, including free childcare and transportation.

They later wrote about us in their 2008 book *Our Lives Out Loud:* "What impressed us most ... was how the friendship shared between Rosemary and Nancy and between all the members of the community provided a relational power effective enough to develop new social and economic systems for the towns and cities of Massachusetts. Subsequently, we often sat at their table, having meals with the guests who had been homeless. We gathered by their fireside to reflect with guests, members of the community and public-policy experts on lessons learned from their work within a setting of mutual respect, care and shared resources. We witnessed conflict—its resolution, its hardship. We felt the potency of faithful hope."

CHAPTER 5

Stretching Hospitality

Ann Louise and Katherine told us they recognized on their first visit why people were so attracted to Wellspring House: hospitality. Homeless families, volunteers, donors, neighbors, people with complaints, and those who were simply curious about what we were doing—all were welcomed. We had a matter-of-fact expectation that the natural response to meeting new people was openness and friendliness and often a cup of tea. One did not need to spell it out. But we were not naïve. Whenever you invite a new element in your life, whether a person or an idea, you make yourself vulnerable and allow yourself to be turned in a direction you hadn't foreseen. Hospitality has risks and also must have limits for the sake of both host and guest.

Right away we recognized that the answer to the increasing numbers of homeless families was not more shelters but permanent affordable housing. So we focused on finding permanent housing for our guests. We didn't really have a choice. If we were going to have homeless people in our home, we could not keep them forever. People would often say to us, It's so beautiful here. Your guests are never going to want to leave. But they wanted to leave. They wanted their own places.

Most social-service organizations have one thing they do, one service they provide, then they grow that into a larger organization. We were committed to listening to our guests tell us what *they* needed to rise out of poverty and realize their dreams, then helping them find it—certainly affordable housing, but also education, food for their families, and jobs that paid a living wage and would get them off welfare. That was radical for a small organization. How can one do all those things and do them well? We did some better than others. Our own ambitions, as well as requests that came from the community, pushed us to stretch our hospitality.

***

Ron and Shirley were a middle-aged couple who had fallen in love when they were both residents at Danvers State Hospital. Ron suffered from chronic depression, and Shirley's mental illness left her hardly able to express herself verbally. Ron helped her. When the state moved mental-health services out of residential settings to community programs that were still not fully functional, they were suddenly isolated and adrift. Deinstitutionalized patients had no counselor or mental-health worker assigned to them. To stay on their medications, they had to find their own medical doctor. They had a place to stay, but they needed more social interactions and support than they were getting. The nearest social-services office was more than a half hour drive away. That office asked if we could help.

What the couple needed—an ongoing home but for just a few days a week—had never been in our plan, and the logistics were challenging. We had no spare rooms. But for almost a year we welcomed them each weekend to sleep on a pull-out couch on the sunporch, where the television was. Guests had to clear out by eleven on weekends so Ron and Shirley could go to bed. They became part of the weekend rhythm, helping with dishes after meals, doing the Saturday cleaning chores, and joining our Sunday ritual and Thanksgiving and Christmas celebrations with us.

Ron had been discharged from the hospital first, and he loved to tell the story of how he used to hitchhike down Route 1 to visit Shirley. One evening, sitting in the passenger seat of his ride, he reached into his back pocket for his handkerchief and instead pulled out Shirley's panties. Everyone would laugh and laugh, and Shirley would protest, tears running down her cheeks with laughter, "Don't tell that story!" One day Nancy was washing dishes and Ron was drying, and she remarked, "You seem pretty good this weekend." Ron, who was very sociable most of the time, replied soberly, "I can't tell you what it's like to wake up every morning and be depressed and get through the day." Eventually we helped them find subsidized housing, and they always kept in touch. When Ron died some years later, the funeral service was held in the Wellspring chapel.

Hospitality also meant being open to requests and ideas brought to us. On Christmas Eve 1982, just as we were leaving for Midnight Mass, the telephone rang. Mark answered. The Thanksgiving-to-Christmas holiday period was always a time when people thought about those who had less.

The caller was angry that so little was being done to address hunger in Gloucester, and she thought Wellspring should do more. Mark listened and explained we were on our way to services but asked for her number so they could continue the conversation. Just a few days later a group of students from Gordon College on Christmas break stopped in and wanted to talk about setting up a soup kitchen in Gloucester. We hosted a meeting, inviting the students, the woman who had rung on Christmas Eve, some local pastors, members of the Rockport Congregational Church who were already running a food pantry, and representatives from the local Action Inc anti-poverty agency. We were happy to host meetings and support the effort, but we knew we didn't have the resources or people power to take on the project.

Over the next months the planning group decided to increase the hours and step up the amount of food available in the Rockport pantry and to offer a weekly hot-meal program on a trial basis. In November 1983 the group served the first meal to fifteen people at the former senior center in Gloucester. They soon realized the need was greater than they'd thought, both the number of people who were hungry and their individual needs. The people who came needed not only a hot meal but also friendship. They were lonely. They liked eating with others, getting to know one another, and saving seats for their new special friends. Several came early to help set up and chat.

Within a year the volunteer organizers had incorporated a nonprofit called The Open Door—A Place of Hospitality. Just as we avoided calling Wellspring a "shelter," we didn't want it to be called a "soup kitchen." Guests did not stand in line to get their food. Volunteers served them at tables at a new larger space at the Methodist Church in Gloucester, though the church didn't allow us to use its kitchen. So organizers signed up twenty-four teams from other churches, the temple, civic organizations, and nonprofits, including Wellspring, to prepare the food, bring it to the church, set up tables, serve fifty to eighty meals twice weekly, and clean up afterward. Our new organization bought our own set of dishes because we didn't want to use paper plates.

In November 1984 The Open Door board hired Nancy to coordinate the new project, which meant organizing the teams, being on hand at each meal, and raising money. Many of the mostly white, middle-class volunteers weren't used to interacting with people who were poor. They would stiffly offer to take their coats, use formal names like Rev. or Mr or Mrs, and try to instruct them what to do any time they moved—where to get food, where to put their tray and trash. In truth, the guests usually knew more about how things worked than volunteers who showed up only once a quarter. Nancy encouraged the volunteers to relax, just talk to folks, and get to know them. Wellspring House also became the base where volunteers handled the intake calls for the food pantry and the meal program—finding out their names, how many people in a family to expect, how many children, any food restrictions. For more than twenty years Wellspring staff and volunteers worked closely with The Open Door and the food pantry, which merged in 1986.

***

From the beginning our vision was to create a movement of hospitality that could spread and take root. In 1982 Rosemary was invited to speak on a panel at a theology conference at Chicago Theological Union. She really connected with another panelist, Edwina Gateley, also a British lay theologian, who became a dear friend. Edwina was funny, even irreverent, and committed to social justice, all of which we loved. Her work inspired our next project.

Edwina had spent four years in Uganda as a missionary after college. She took a thirty-day solo retreat in the Sahara Desert and discovered *she* was the one converted to a new religious view. "In Africa, my understanding of God changed because of the hospitality, generosity, and openness of the African people," she wrote in her book *In God's Womb*. "Their notion of God seemed to be so much bigger than what I had learned from my church at home. I learned that we are suffused with God."

Full of her African experience and, like us, inspired by the Vatican II teachings about the role of the laity, she went to London to meet with John Heenan, Cardinal Archbishop of Westminster. She proposed her idea of training lay missionaries, not to convert people to Christianity, but to live and learn together and share skills—carpentry, repairs, digging latrines, building, cooking, teaching, whatever local people said they needed. In the

1960s for a young laywoman like Edwina to approach a cardinal, and one who didn't approve of Vatican II at that, was audacious on so many levels. He had a suggestion for her: Go become a nun. She had zero interest in that. She realized she didn't need anyone's blessing or permission.

Through sheer force of will, and little money, she started the Volunteer Missionary Movement in 1969. She heard about a vacant thirty-room house on four acres, outside London, owned by the Archdiocese of Westminster. Boldly, Edwina went back to the Cardinal and asked if she could use it, for free. There were excuses and resistance, but she persisted. Eventually he said yes. In the coming years, her organization trained thousands of volunteers to serve in twenty-six countries on three continents.

In 1979 she stepped down as leader to get her master's degree in theology at Chicago Theological Union. In Chicago, Edwina began to understand her mission was to serve the street people she saw, women who were homeless, addicted to drugs, and sex workers. She spent 1983 walking the streets with sex workers at night and visiting brothels as part of her fieldwork. "One night I was walking with one of the prostitutes along Sheridan Road just north of where I live," Edwina told the *Chicago Tribune*, "when someone started throwing stones at us and calling us whores. Just then, at that moment, I knew what it was like to be scorned as a prostitute. It was also the moment when I felt closest to God. I could almost envision Jesus preventing the stoning of a prostitute by an angry mob by challenging the man without sin to cast the first stone .... I knew that I had to provide a place for these women to get away to an oasis of safety and calm away from the mind-numbing violence, hypocrisy, and sexual abuse of the streets." One madam gave her $100 a month to help with her expenses.

The next year she found a three-story walk-up near Wrigley Field and called it Genesis House as a place of hospitality for sex workers. Over the next ten years it became home for five or six women at a time who wanted to quit their addictions and sex work, and many others stopped in for coffee and chats. Judges who had been sending sex workers to prison started sending them to Genesis House instead.

Edwina adopted a 3-day-old boy born to a Genesis House woman who was trying to get clean but did not survive the birth. She named him Niall, Gaelic for champion, and Kizito for his East African heritage. She so disliked most of the religious education materials for children that she started writing and illustrating a series of books about the God she believed in, a funny, curious God who wanted to go on picnics, to the beach, on vacation, and have fun with people, not just be with them when they dressed up on Sundays, sang serious songs, and kept quiet. She made her living writing books and leading retreats, though some dioceses would not let her come for her expansive view of God and her irrepressible habit of tweaking the church.

She accepted our invitation to serve on the Wellspring board and made us a cute cartoon about the Parable of the Loaves and Fishes, where one of the apostles says, "They want ketchup." For years it hung on the Wellspring House kitchen wall.

Edwina was much on our minds when we decided we, too, wanted to train and send people to work in places with extreme poverty around the country. Over the years the two of us had visited laypeople and nuns living with people in these places. We knew they would welcome our recruits. Our idea was that the host organizations would help our Wellspring trainees find rental or donated housing as their home base, then they could use their skills on the most pressing local need, and draw in other volunteers, as we had done at Wellspring.

During the month-long training before they set out, the whole Wellspring community, including guests, took part in sharing meals and ideas. Local friends hosted the trainees in their homes. We used Gloucester as a subject for analysis. Walking through the city, the trainees had the first impression that Gloucester was very middle class. There were no visible signs of poverty. However, as they volunteered in local agencies such as Action Inc, the Housing Authority, and The Open Door, they came to understand that the causes of poverty in Gloucester were the same as in other places: the gap between income and the cost of living.

***

This gap had widened in Gloucester by the collapse of the fishing industry. Gloucester calls itself the oldest fishing port in America, ever since a handful of British fishermen started a commercial cod-fishing business in 1623. Dramatic stories of Gloucester fishing families have been the subject of films like *The Perfect Storm, CODA*, and the 1937 *Captains Courageous*, based on Rudyard Kipling's book and earning Spencer Tracy an Oscar. But today the family-fishing fleet has been reduced to a few handfuls of boats. Whale-watching boats based in the harbor are what attracts tourists. They also flock to see the iconic Fishermen's Memorial statue, dedicated to the 10,000 Gloucester fishermen who have lost their lives.

In the late twentieth century, a series of short-sighted federal policies devastated the US fishing industry, especially smaller family-fishing boat owners like those in Gloucester. In the 1960s the federal government, alarmed by enormous Soviet trawlers scouring the ocean floor close to US waters and processing their catch on board, increased the "exclusive economic zone" reserved for American fishing from just 3 miles to 200. It also incentivized Americans to maximize fishing, offering loans to finance large commercial steel ships like the Soviets'. In a matter of years, those US-based trawlers had predictably overfished the richest fishing grounds, like Georges Bank off New England, which Gloucester fishing families in their smaller wooden boats had depended on for centuries. Federal regulators stepped in again with quotas, zone limits, limits on days or hours to fish, and regulations on the size of fish and net mesh.

Fishing families in Gloucester were furious and insulted. Who cared more about the sea than they did? Who knew better? Primarily of Sicilian and Portuguese ancestry, the women in the families, who stayed onshore shopping and managing their households, spoke better English than their husbands. These fishermen's wives argued at endless meetings and hearings, insisting that government scientists go out on their boats to see for themselves. They were so respected throughout the city. Lena Novello, the formidable mama of the fishermen's wives who always dyed her hair an arresting dark black, would stand up and say: "You don't know a thing you're talking about. Do you know who rules the ocean? Jesus rules the ocean."

These families also took immense pride in their homes. The exteriors always looked neat, with well-tended vegetable and flower gardens, hiding the angst, anger, and poverty within. Many in Gloucester were losing their boats, their businesses, and their homes. Not only fishing families but all who supported the industry: ice companies, net makers, boat builders, fish processors, and many more. When they did lose their homes, the extended families did not want their women going to Wellspring. They believed the family should take care of its own, though many families simply could not. We had to be extremely sensitive in how we offered our hospitality.

***

At that time Gloucester did not have people living on the streets. We took our trainees in our Mission for a North American Movement program down to the waterfront to hear from the lumpers who unloaded the fish off the boats. We walked around Portuguese Hill, topped off by Our Lady of Good Voyage Church, and among the lovely painted houses in the Italian neighborhood with their shrines, and talked to neighbors. We went into the Veterans Memorial School, which taught kids from lower-income neighborhoods, and heard from the principal and teachers about kids who didn't have enough to eat or clothes to wear. We went into The Open Door. There we met mothers with young children who sometimes didn't like the food but more often asked for more, elderly people who were hungry and lonely, and young men, even teenagers, who were embarrassed to be there. We went into the Housing Authority and Action Inc and saw desperate people seeking housing and fuel assistance being told the wait list for Section 8 federal housing vouchers—which helped families with very low incomes, the elderly, and people with disabilities pay for housing in the private market—was two years.

Each afternoon the trainees returned to Wellspring, and we would reflect together on what they observed and learned. Our reflection included study of Mark's gospel showing how Jesus responded to suffering with compassion and by sharing food and life and work, such as the parable that Edwina illustrated for us, where he fed 5,000 with two loaves and five fishes. Jesus called the people he served friends, who together could release the power of God's justice. He was preaching "Power With," not the "Power Over" practiced by Rome.

We used Paulo Freire's process of action, then reflection. One or two trainees would present. They might say: "It was hard for me. I felt this worker was being harsh. I wanted to jump in." Or: "I went to The Open Door and couldn't believe there was so much need for food. People really are poor." By working in agencies where people were being helped, the trainees got to observe both people who needed help and people whose jobs were to help. They saw the approach of some government agencies versus people like Peter Anastas at Action Inc, one of the most compassionate intake workers. He treated people like his community or friends, not clients: "Hey, I see you live here. Do you know this person? Maybe you could try this landlord. I hear they had an opening." Then we talked about how the trainees would change their day, what they could do differently, and how they wanted their next day to go.

At the end of the month some of the trainees decided not to continue, but most worked for two years. Some went to Edwina's Genesis House in Chicago to work with sex workers, the most homeless of all women. They were the rejects, the despised, used, and often soon dead. Some went to teach literacy to immigrants in Gary, Indiana, where the collapse of the steel industry had left empty, rusting mills, many people unemployed, and a permanent yellow fog enveloping the city. The classrooms were so cold they all had to wear coats and gloves inside and could hardly hold their pencils. Some went to the coal regions of Kentucky and West Virginia, where extraordinary natural beauty was the background to extreme poverty and exploitation. One trainee in West Virginia worked on establishing a domestic violence shelter for women in a culture that regarded wife beating as normal. She helped the women go to court to get restraining orders against their husbands.

The two of us visited these MNAM workers to see how they were doing. They were people of remarkable courage and ingenuity. But it was hard, lonely, and sometimes depressing work, confronting a degree of poverty they could never fully address. Their host communities provided a place to live, emotional support, and mentoring. But we didn't have funds for stipends, so they had to find work or outside funding to support themselves.

After three years we ended the program. Everyone involved felt it had been valuable, both the training and the work. But we realized we had taken it on too early, before we had established our funding sources. Family homelessness was reaching a crisis point, and we simply did not have the resources to work on both.

***

At the same time our resident community was dwindling. The RCE order had reassigned Jenny to other work, to her regret. In 1983, having completed her doctorate, Marygrace was working as a family counselor.. While attending a conference in Western Massachusetts, she heard a voice call out: "Sister Marygrace!" It was Don Hommen, a former pastor of St John's Lutheran in Peabody, whom she had worked with when she was president of the city's interfaith association. She told him: "I'm not Sister Marygrace anymore. I'm Marygrace." They fell in love at once. For four nights Nancy tried to reach her by phone, but there was no answer. "She's met someone," Nancy told Rosemary. On the last night Nancy finally got through: "Did you meet someone!" Surprised, Marygrace replied: "Nan, how did you know?" Don and Marygrace soon made plans to marry, and Mark also announced he would be marrying Margaret Rose, another Episcopal priest. Rosemary made the wedding dresses for both brides. Margaret's was cut down from a much larger dress of her sister's, with a big train. Marygrace's was from a Vogue pattern, with a lace appliqué made by Carol Provenzano around the hem.

That summer while we were visiting Rosemary's family in England, a former Catholic priest and his wife needed a place to stay in Massachusetts, and we offered them our rooms. Surrounded by Rosemary's books, he had a psychotic break. He threw all her books off the shelves, set them on fire, and locked himself in the room. Paul was able to open the door and use the fire extinguisher. The old wooden house was saved from going up in a flash, but most of our possessions were destroyed. When the firefighters arrived, they asked, "Is there anything precious upstairs?" Mary Jane shrieked, "The wedding gown in the closet!" When Marygrace picked us up at the airport, we were anxious to get home, but she said, "Let's stop for dinner." Nancy protested, "I don't want to." Marygrace, who was driving, said, "Well, I do." She told us there was nothing left of our things, all our clothes, everything was gone. But the wedding dress was saved. Marygrace and Don were married in a beautiful ceremony in September.

Both Marygrace and Mark moved out of Wellspring to new homes with their partners but remained active for years, serving on the board and in many other ways. Mark often brought his Morris dancing set to Wellspring for our celebrations. Then in 1985 we lost Jenny. She became

Stretching Hospitality

ill with cancer, which progressed rapidly. At her request Mark sang for her in the last hours of her life.

The Wellspring community also experienced births, giving us the chance to offer a delightful kind of hospitality. In 1982 Sissy's sister, Heidi, gave birth to baby Naomi in the birthing center of the local hospital, accompanied by her boyfriend. Heidi and Naomi came home to Wellspring that night. Another baby soon followed: Gail, a guest in the house, had a baby daughter, Lindsay. Our photo album shows her at about a year old, trying unsuccessfully to drink from a mug—reminding us of how long they and other families had to wait on affordable-housing lists.

The shortage of affordable housing shaped the way Wellspring developed in the following years. Demand was so great we needed to put even more limits on the guests we accepted. We still welcomed fathers of children who were homeless, but we no longer accepted single men. We were seeing more and more need for homes for single women, many who had been abused and were intimidated by the presence of men. Sadly, too, many of the single men wanted to touch the women, pinch them, use inappropriate language, and shout at their kids to move or shut up. The women predictably fought back whenever the men spoke harshly to their children. One man came just for meals for a while. Everyone loved him, and at heart he was a good man. But when he showed up drunk, he harassed the women terribly. We had to tell him not to come back. Those kinds of situations were so touchy, and we had so much to learn. At one point Ellen Kelly gave him some money. Nancy told her, a bit too preachily, "You mustn't do that." Ellen, who had been a heavy drinker in the past and knew him from the bars, called Nancy out on the spot: "You know I like you. But you sure can't talk to me that way. You don't know who he is in my life and what we've done for each other. Don't ever tell me again how to spend my money." And she was right. In 1983 Action Inc opened a shelter for single people so we could refer single men there.

To help our guests feel more secure, we let them know they could knock on our door if they needed help in the night. One pregnant woman, Kayla, had left her abusive husband and come to Wellspring with her little boy. She was very religious and felt guilty about leaving her husband. She was also afraid he would come after her and take her son. She couldn't sleep.

One night she knocked, shivering with fear, and Rosemary came and sat on her bed and read comforting Bible passages till she fell asleep. Nancy accompanied her to the hospital when her baby girl, Jocinda, was born prematurely and nearly died. Kayla and her children were later supported by her church. For years mother and daughter brought Nancy an African violet on Jocinda's birthday.

What we were experiencing was part of a wider crisis. The phenomenon of families being made homeless was in full force in the early 1980s, a direct outcome of Reaganomics and the cuts in all federal programs. The already limited supply of Section 8 federal housing vouchers was drastically reduced, as well as federal money to maintain current public housing and produce more. At Wellspring we knew firsthand that families were homeless not because they were "lazy," as some politicians described them. Simply, they did not have the money. We heard stories of the lengths that women went to avoid being homeless: working multiple jobs, getting training and more education, couch surfing, living with parents, jumping into new relationships, with great promises but too often worse than the one they were in. The women we met were at the end of their ropes.

Like the laywomen who had started the RCE order after the French Revolution, religious organizations and grassroots groups like ours sprang up to fill the gap, providing beds and meals so people would not freeze in the winter or live in their cars. But helping families move out of shelter and into homes was a daunting job. We assisted our families at Wellspring fill out their applications for Section 8 vouchers. But the wait list was long to get a voucher, then even longer to find an eligible rental. Meanwhile, we had to turn away other homeless families. We made connections with a few local landlords who owned low-cost rental housing and weren't leaping to convert them to condominiums. Whenever we secured a rental for one of our families, Wellspring volunteers helped mend doors and windows, paint, hang blinds, and find donated furniture. In one unit, we opened a window, and the whole thing fell out. We replaced it. Gail and Lindsay were among those lucky ones to get one of these units, however basic, and it was a day of celebration when they finally had a home of their own.

In many ways, we were fortunate to be in Massachusetts. Both state government and nonprofit leaders recognized that shelters alone would not solve the state's rapidly growing homeless problem. The Massachusetts Coalition for the Homeless, created as a nonprofit in 1981, had 1,400 members by 1983. The goal was to *solve* the problem, not simply to manage it. The coalition analyzed and named the causes of homelessness in the state: lack of housing, deinstitutionalization of mental-health services, alcohol and drug abuse, domestic violence, and family turmoil. In his inaugural speech as governor in January 1983, Michael Dukakis named homelessness as his top social priority. Later that year he signed the Act to Prevent Destitution and Homelessness, known as Chapter 450 of 1983. Four state departments—Community Development, Public Welfare, Human Services, and Mental Health—were charged to work together on a solution. In addition to emergency services like shelters, the solution would require prevention of all the causes the coalition had named, support for homeless people as they sought homes, and permanent affordable housing to move into.

Even though we preferred not to call Wellspring a shelter or a social-service agency—and thought of ourselves as a community offering hospitality to people in crisis—we needed to think about how we fit into the statewide system. Patrick Walsh, head of the Homeless Division of the state Welfare Department, encouraged us to apply for a contract for shelter services with the state in the mid-1980s. After months of discussions, our board decided to apply for a state contract for 60 percent of shelter costs. It also voted that Wellspring would always limit itself to 60 percent for any future state-funded programs we applied for. We did not want to lose our identity. We had seen other vital local programs funded by the state abruptly ended when the political winds changed. We wanted always to have a base of funds to build on.

The contract enabled us to help homeless families financially at a level that had previously been impossible because our guests now had access to a state emergency assistance fund. We helped them navigate applications to help pay for overdue rent, utility bills, furniture storage, and moving costs. We also had access to state-funded Chapter 707 rental subsidies, in addition to the federal Section 8 vouchers. That meant families could find housing in as little as six to eight weeks. Wellspring could pay salaries to Nancy, Rosemary, and Mary Jane as case managers—we could give up our outside part-time jobs, though Rosemary continued writing and lecturing. Nancy became the shelter program coordinator. And we hired staff for two new required positions: a housing search coordinator and a family life advocate.

As huge as those changes were for our little organization, the state contract made little difference to daily life at Wellspring. We had always welcomed homeless people, and we continued to cook, eat family-style meals, clean, and create a beautiful home together. The drawbacks of the contract were minor. Previously we had asked guests who received government benefits to contribute a small amount, which helped with our tight budget and gave them some dignity. The state contract did not allow this, and we could take only guests who were referred to us by the Department of Public Welfare. If people came to the door or were referred by local organizations or churches, the way they always had, we had to send them to the department's local office first. There was also some extra record keeping and form filling to submit our monthly bill to the state.

Most importantly, the needs of the families were still at the center of our day-to-day decisions. The bureaucratic culture at the Department of Public Welfare assumed homeless people were responsible for their situation. "Lazy" was still a common explanation, but "depression" became a new attempt to locate a cause. Recent research had shown that homeless women were likely depressed and had concluded that homelessness was a mental-health problem rather than an economic one, and that homeless women were passive and incompetent. Our experience was that if homeless women were depressed, it was *because* of their homelessness, not the other way around. These families were homeless, quite simply, because they couldn't afford to rent. Almost all were doing their best to cope. Their "depression" was appropriate. Families coming into shelters were in the middle of the worst kind of crisis. Most were single-parent families headed by women. They had lost their homes and often their furniture. Most of all they had lost control over their lives and were dependent on the decisions of strangers. Their children were often upset and insecure. The mothers tried to comfort and reassure them, while blaming themselves and feeling they had failed. They often came to us quite reasonably angry and sometimes suspicious that we were profiting by sheltering them. We did what we could to make them feel safe and welcome, making their rooms as pretty and comfortable as possible with fresh bed linens and curtains, thoroughly cleaned and spotless when they arrived. They and their children had freedom to use the common rooms of the beautiful old house and could play or sit in the garden or under the trees in the shady yard. The structure of the household—regular mealtimes for all, bedtimes for children according to age, and shared cooking and cleaning—was often initially hard for families to accept. Once the children were all in bed, the women could come down to the sunporch and socialize, relax in front of the television, or fill out housing applications together. Many had never set fixed bedtimes nor had time with women friends. They found their children thrived, and so did they. The understandable resentment and defensiveness usually faded. When a new home became a real possibility and then a fact, their "depression" lifted and was replaced with hope and energy.

Each of us worked with individual families as "case managers," as we were called in welfare language, a title we felt demeaned the women. We helped them navigate the system to get income, housing, childcare, and health care. In weekly group meetings our housing search advocate Donna Leria helped parents with the overwhelming business of putting together a housing "portfolio," which included separate housing applications to each town's Housing Authority, applications for subsidies, and letters of recommendation.

Having a neighborhood elementary school, West Parish, in walking distance, as well as city-run early-childhood and after-school programs nearby, made a huge quality-of-life difference both to our children and to parents, who were usually working or in school themselves. West Parish School welcomed Wellspring children whenever they enrolled in the school year, even if only for a few months. At that time many shelters didn't have the resources to get children enrolled short-term. West Parish Principal Jim Gutstadt sometimes stopped in to Wellspring for lunch. The children would proudly whisper, "That's my principal!" Whenever a child was moving on to a new home, Jim would announce it to the whole school in an assembly, saying, "I've got some really good news!" At the end of the day he would ring the bell and gather the children and teachers in the entryway to cheer and send off the family.

***

One of the terms we insisted on in our state contract was allowing Wellspring to shelter boys over age 12 along with their families, which no other shelter did. Teenage boys had to go to a men's shelter. One such family came to us in the late 1990s, a Puerto Rican mother who had been chronically homeless, with a young daughter and a 16-year-old son. Carlos was full of suspicion of do-gooders but also had tremendous resilience, intelligence, imagination, and curiosity. We gave him his own room, a precious experience in a life of constant moving from filthy borrowed couches or in with drug-dealing friends.

While living at Wellspring, Carlos attended Gloucester High School, where principal Joseph Sullivan mentored him. A Wellspring staff member, Rachel, also took an interest in him, as she did with many residents, asking questions and genuinely listening. "She was an artsy redhead who exuded life," Carlos later remembered. "We'd talk about anything from goblins to God, and she introduced me to tea with milk. She was something between a therapist and an older sister." One night she handed Carlos a wrapped gift. It was a black hardcover journal and a pencil. Carlos began to write. That was a turning point for him. He could put down all his thoughts, unfiltered, and evaluate them. "It never cared if I sounded stupid or vain or whiny or sentimental," he later wrote. "It was a barometer of my mental-health, a promise my present made to my future."

That year Nancy was named one of the Heroes Among Us by the Boston Celtics basketball team. She asked Carlos's mother if she could invite him as her plus-one to the game. The Celtics sent a car to pick them up for the thirty-mile trip into the Boston Garden arena. Carlos couldn't believe he'd be seeing his heroes in person. When Nancy was called down from their center court seats at half time, she asked Carlos, who had a recently broken leg still in a cast, to join her on the court with the team.

Carlos did not want his classmates to know that he lived in a homeless shelter. The school bus always stopped right across from Wellspring House to pick up students. But Carlos chose to walk the two miles to school in his orange Doc Martens, gold chains swinging from his neck. When his family found a new home in Connecticut later in the school year, he wrote his classmates a letter. He first showed it to his English teacher, Natalie Daley, and she encouraged him to read it to his classmates. *The Gloucester*

Times heard about it and also wrote a story about the family, publishing the letter alongside. Here's an excerpt: "All this time we've been in school together, joked together, you've been sharing it with a homeless person. Yes, homeless, I can imagine the looks on your faces right now ... What a shock, huh? ... Before coming here I thought of the risks of inequality I'd face ... being Hispanic, coming from a place where people talk and dress different would set me apart .... I am really no different than you .... This letter isn't for you to pity me or even to regret anything you said to me in the past. This letter is to ask you to open your eyes, to see people for who they are and not for who they hang with, where they come from, what race they are or how they dress. This letter is for the next kid who comes to your city, your school, with my secret—homelessness. Just stop a minute and think about how society has taught us to think about such things."

The next ten years of his life were very difficult. Carlos used and dealt drugs and became part of a gang that stole cars and took them across the state line to sell. Eventually he was caught and arrested, convicted, and sentenced to time in prison. In prison he had more time to reflect, write in his journal, and took advantage of therapy offered there. He remembered the times in his life when someone had been kind to him, cared for him, respected him, and affirmed him. The real Carlos started to come alive again. He realized that all he had been through "has made me pretty good at understanding other people and how to help them and that 'Your gift is what you give away,'" he wrote, paraphrasing Pablo Picasso. "This was how everything I had been through could be turned to good. It was why I was still alive despite everything, and it was why I was going to write my book."

Once out of prison, he found a decent job with a loan company, which eventually sent him to Iowa to start a new branch. He trained to be a coach and mentor for troubled men and women, and today he does public speaking and produces digital media for his own company called Ghetto To Greatness (GTG) Media.

Carlos published his book in 2021, called *The Resurrection Plant: Your Pain Is Your Path to Greatness*. The image of the desert plant that can survive years of drought by curling into a lifeless ball, then bursts into life and blooms when touched by water, is a fitting metaphor for Carlos's own journey, how a little kindness and hope can turn a life from desolation to love. A chapter in the book recalls the months he spent at Wellspring—the first time he had his own room, the first time he felt safe when he got in bed at night. His message is that people need to be told, shown, and know in their hearts: they're lovable, they're loved, and they can love other people. We couldn't agree more.

 A few years ago while in Gloucester for a wedding, he visited us and brought us a copy of his book. Knocking at our door, he had tears streaming down his face. Nancy still had the Boston Celtics trophy. She handed it to him, saying, "I want you to have this. You're the hero."

CHAPTER 6

Housing Should Be a Right

Early in 1984 a local landlord, Frank Sclafani, phoned us. "I have a property that will help you girls do your work." We were in our 40s and 50s, but we let that go. "My wife and I own a lodging house at 99 Washington Street that we will rent to you. All it needs is a lick of paint! Would you like to see it?"

Mary Jane and Nancy met him at the house. It needed a lot more than a lick of paint. The first and second floors each had two units, with a bathroom to share. The toilets on both floors were broken. The third floor had two dormer rooms, no bathroom. There was no hot water. City inspectors had required light fixtures in the hallways, but the fixtures had never been connected to electricity. And there was a lot of general dirt.

But Mary Jane, who along with Paul had rehabbed a triple-decker in a nearby city when they were first married, saw possibilities. The third floor could be built out to make two complete additional units, along with some storage—bringing the total units to six, which could be used as transitional housing for families waiting for subsidies or affordable housing for women with just one or two children. And Mary Jane was a pretty good negotiator.

"I don't think Wellspring will rent the house in its present condition, but would you consider selling it to us?" she began her negotiation.

Mr Sclafani thought for a minute. "I'm open to that, but I will have to check with my wife. Rosalie really wants to hold on to our rental properties for income."

Mary Jane said, "If she agrees, do you have an idea of your ballpark sale price?"

He replied, "I think about $100,000, but again I will have to confirm that with Rosalie."

Then Mary Jane asked a third question: "If your wife agrees to sell, and to your price, would you consider holding the mortgage?"

He answered: "I will talk with Rosalie and get back to you."

She explained that we would need the information for the board meeting "next week." The timing was actually perfect for us. At the end of 1983 our Finance Committee had happily projected a $10,000 surplus in the budget for the next year. They recommended starting a Housing Fund that would make affordable housing an explicit part of our mission, which endured for the next twenty-five years. It was a radical commitment for such a small organization. We would have had a hard time coming up with any down payment without that surplus.

The next afternoon he rang to say they would sell us the building and hold the $100,000 mortgage at 10 percent for twenty years, a pretty good deal at that time, with bank interest rates at about 14 percent. At a special board meeting, the board voted to explore the possibility of buying and then rehabbing the house. Our finance committee, with Fred Hoffman as chair, got busy with setting up building inspections and estimating the rehab and operating costs, getting bids for builders, plumbers, and electricians. At the end of March, Wellspring signed a purchase and sales agreement and made a down payment of $10,000, using all our newly established housing fund.

Shortly after, we saw a notice that the Gloucester Grants Administration office was hosting a meeting about affordable-housing rehab. Nancy and Mary Jane walked into the meeting, the only attendees, and told the two staff members our plans. They seemed excited to have attendees, and their office ultimately signed an agreement to loan Wellspring $50,000, most of the cost of the rehab. Wellspring agreed to rent five units to low-income tenants and meet other operating standards. If we complied, the loan would be forgiven at the end of ten years. We also received a $10,000 grant from The Fund for the Homeless, set up in 1983 by Massachusetts First Lady Kitty Dukakis, for capital improvements to shelters. We learned Mrs Dukakis was very pleased to help a shelter that also wanted to develop affordable housing.

On a beautiful autumn day in October 1984 we celebrated the opening of the transformed apartments and invited people from state and city departments, carpenters, plumbers—everybody who worked on it in any way—for a tour and lunch at a waterfront restaurant. Frank and Rosalie Sclafani came from New York City, where they had since retired, and received a standing ovation. Bill Dugan, head of the Gloucester Housing Authority, told those gathered: "The lights had gone out on the possibility of affordable housing in Gloucester, until this small group of people moved in and said, 'It's possible!'"

We moved two homeless families from Wellspring House and three single women on our waiting list into the five apartments. We hired Donna Leria, who later served as our housing search coordinator, as the live-in manager in the sixth unit. A remarkable young woman, Donna had her first child at age 18 and had lived in Cambridge with three other young single mothers. They shared childcare so they could work. She had a way of seeing and lifting up people's strengths—noticing how they kept their apartment clean, or their sense of humor, or that they followed through on what they said they'd do. She would ask the women questions and truly listen: "What do you want for your life?" They wanted their own place. Donna would ask: "What would that take?" Saving money. Donna: "How much can you save each week?" Then she would check in with them. If they fell short, she'd ask: "What would it take so you can meet your goal next week or next month?" She insisted on getting play equipment and a grill and encouraged the tenants to hang out in the backyard, celebrate birthdays together, and eat together. She herself hosted dinners out of her tiny kitchen. She got to know local landlords, knew which ones had Section 8 vouchers, and which ones to avoid. The landlords trusted her references. If any of her former tenants had issues in their new homes, she would go with them to help sort it out.

The experience of developing affordable housing at 99 Washington Street was a steep learning curve for our little group of mostly educators and church people. We had to master all the real-world details of design, electrical systems, plumbing, and permits. When Nancy was asked to speak to state agencies and groups in future years, she often said, "There is no mystery to how to develop affordable housing. It is simply the lack of imagination and the will to take on the many challenges involved and do it."

We were always preaching that imagination is a critical tool in social transformation. Certainly it didn't take much imagination to see what the problem was. For what the state spent on shelters—and this is still true today—numerous affordable-housing units could be built. It was a question of allocating already available resources and sitting down and imagining a different solution. We knew firsthand how desperately both families and single people needed permanent affordable housing. That was the only real solution to homelessness, and we were committed to doing whatever it took to develop more.

***

Our very first guest, Ellen, had moved out of Wellspring but to a precarious life. In the winter she rented a room in a guest house at the off-season rate on the wild and rocky Back Shore of Gloucester facing the Atlantic Ocean. When the summer tenants returned after Memorial Day, Ellen had to vacate. She didn't have any camping equipment, but the owners of the Cape Ann Campground let her sleep in a cinderblock room in the building where the laundry and bathrooms were. Every evening she'd walk a couple of miles each way to have dinner at Wellspring House.

Ellen taught us so much about the many jobless, vulnerable, and often traumatized single women who are so marginalized they are almost invisible, surviving in the corners. We tried to help her find a job. Even with all her best intentions and the goodwill of understanding employers, she could not hold a job. She always showed up on time for her jobs in a nursing home laundry or a motel kitchen, but she just could not concentrate. We referred her to a therapist who diagnosed several mental-health issues, including post-traumatic stress syndrome from growing up in foster care and having to fend for herself at a young age in ways we couldn't even imagine. For years Social Security had turned down her disability applications. Mary Jane and Marygrace helped her appeal. A sympathetic judge ruled in her favor, including back payments since her first application, which added up to about $25,000. Mary Jane was Ellen's representative payee, to help her manage banking and bill paying.

We adored Ellen. She loved cooking and eating food, celebrating holidays, watching movies, and singing along with Mark, especially all the songs from musicals she knew by heart. Years of abuse and neglect may have beaten Ellen down but could not take away her big heart, her love of fun, and her loyalty to her friends. The first thing Ellen did with her money was throw a big party for all her old and new friends at Augustine's Italian restaurant on Route 1 in Saugus. Dressed in a new shirt and blue V-neck sweater that Mary Jane helped her choose, she greeted each of her guests. Her dream was to visit New York City, and for three years in a row one of us accompanied her for a long weekend. She loved going to the theatre, ordering steak in restaurants, and loudly demanding a free refill of her morning coffee, which was the custom in Gloucester but not the city. On one visit she wanted to go to Tiffany's to buy a crystal to hang in her apartment. Mary Jane had made sure she was well dressed in a new coat and slacks, with her hair freshly washed. But the salespeople, fawning over a large group of Japanese tourists on a buying spree, ignored her. Ellen took a quarter out of her pocket, rapped it on the glass counter, and called out loudly, "Sir! May I ask you a question? How much is that watch, right there?" He told her $500. "You've got to be shitting me!" She took her watch off. "I got this in Gloucester, Massachusetts, and it's every bit as good as that watch. You know how much I paid? $100!" Another time when we were coming back to Penn Station, Ellen went with the taxi driver to get our luggage out of the trunk. A man jumped in the front and snatched the driver's money. Lightning-fast, Ellen grabbed him by the coat and hissed: "Don't you ever do anything like that. You know, that's my friend in there," indicating Nancy in the back seat.

Ellen was always in our minds as we undertook our next affordable-housing project. In the 1960s before so-called urban renewal, Gloucester had many boarding houses, where single people could rent a tiny bedroom by the week for something like $20. By the 1980s only a handful of such boarding houses were left. The owner of one at 11 Chestnut Street called to ask if Wellspring wanted to buy it. We did but couldn't commit without securing funding for acquisition, rehabilitation, and operating costs. They responded by lowering the purchase price by $9,000. What we were learning was that with every financial break or receipt of generosity we got, people in the community heard about it, and that unleashed more resources. Each little spark of generosity seemed to light a fire in the hearts of others. We let people know we believed they were the kind of person who does good things: Here's a chance, and we know you'd like to be part of it. And we meant it. (Nancy was especially good at that, Rosemary points out.) Asked to speak at the Christmas party of the Cape Ann Chamber of Commerce,

Nancy mentioned the new affordable-housing opportunity. Paul Sylva, a Rockport businessman who was selling his art-reproduction store—which later gave us beautiful prints to hang at Wellspring House—was looking for a place to invest that cash. He reckoned he could get at least the same return on his investment by lending to Wellspring as the banks would give him. "This could work for both of us," he said. His $70,000 loan covered much of the rehab. As a gesture of support, five local banks agreed to hold a joint mortgage, an unusual arrangement. Wellspring closed on 11 Chestnut Street in May 1986.

The building—close to the shops, cafes, and a laundromat on Main Street and wedged between two other properties—consisted of eight single rooms and a first-floor apartment with a kitchen for a manager. Only one toilet flushed, the showers didn't work, and the sinks had only cold water. The tenants kept illegal hot plates and open tins of food in their filthy rooms, which had cracked linoleum floors, stained torn mattresses, and no bed linens. Roaches went boldly everywhere. There was no fire escape. We had to go to court with the neighbors to get a few feet of easement to make room for one. Just as at 99 Washington Street, we shuddered to think what life inside had been like for them.

We had hoped to convert the building for the many single women we knew who needed homes, like Ellen. But we learned fair-housing laws prohibited us from displacing the five remaining male tenants. So we decided to provide rooms for women on the second floor and men on the third floor, each using one of the two staircases. We turned the manager's apartment kitchen into a common kitchen, something all the tenants expressed a need for. Architects Linda Suter and Shelly Burton donated their services and came up with a plan that gave us ten single rooms and a two-bedroom apartment.

With this purchase, we decided to pursue the state's Chapter 707 program, which provided vouchers that subsidized the building, not the individual tenants' rents, the way the federal Section 8 program did. The Gloucester Housing Authority agreed to administer the vouchers—and still does—and to supervise the rehab. We would own and manage the property.

One of the conditions of converting to a Chapter 707 project was that Wellspring had to provide temporary lodgings for the men during the renovation. But one man never moved out. He had been sick for some time, in a cold room with little furniture, with very occasional deliveries of food by friends. When he dragged himself to the toilet, he left a trail of blood. We found a doctor to do a home visit, who immediately called an ambulance to transport him to the hospital. He died two days later. Once again, we were sobered by the tragedy of destitute single people without family or community services.

Before the rehab began in June 1987, we tried to keep the place decent. Each week Nancy cleaned the bathrooms, swept the hallways and stairways, and told the guys what had to go out of their rooms. They were tenants, not guests like at Wellspring, so we couldn't force them to clean. When Nancy got back to Wellspring House, Mary Jane met her in the carport with new clothes and wouldn't let her in till she had changed. Mary Jane knew roaches. "I've had too much experience with those damn things hiding in the cuffs and creases!"

Nancy got to know the men and asked for their ideas. They were great guys. We got them rooms at the Crow's Nest nearby, the hard-drinking bar made famous in the movie *The Perfect Storm*. The owner was thrilled to have five guaranteed rents. As the tenants were packing up, Ernie met Nancy in the driveway and said, "I'll be moving on. You won't want the likes of me around when the house is all done up and new." Nancy responded, "Ernie, of course, we want you. We're doing the rehab for you!" Ernie said his friends in town told him not to trust us, saying, "They'll double the rent on you." Nancy persuaded him to move to the Crow's Nest and then come back and "try it out" at Chestnut Street. He did and remained our tenant until he moved into nursing home care.

Each Saturday morning Nancy went to the Crow's Nest to pay the rent to the bartender, the mother of Bobby Shatford, a fisherman who died on the *Andrea Gail* in 1991, portrayed by Mark Wahlberg in *The Perfect Storm*. One Saturday a Wellspring supporter rang the house, and Mary Jane answered the phone. The caller said she was afraid Nancy had a drinking problem because every Saturday she saw her go into the Crow's Nest and she was in there for a while. Mary Jane couldn't wait to tell Nancy, screaming with laughter. Life in a small city.

Finally, the renovation was complete, with new bathrooms, rugs, and curtains, good-quality washable mattresses with sheets and blankets, and freshly painted second-hand chests. For the first time the house had color: blues, greens, and oranges, and pretty patterns on the textiles. There were free laundry machines in the basement, and we urged our tenants to do a wash at least every two weeks. The common kitchen had new appliances and a cabinet with a lock for each tenant. One of the tenants, Harold, planted a garden in the front of the house that he tended for years and each Thanksgiving cooked dinner for everyone. We invited neighbors over for a tour, answered their questions, and allayed their concerns about a lodging house with ten tenants, both men and women. The first tenants moved in, and we had an open house on December 4, 1987.

That was a very special day for all of us. Ellen Kelly moved into the largest room on the second floor, at the front of the house, giving her the comfort and security of her own place for the first time in her life.

***

Realtors were now calling to offer us properties that were "just right" for us. We were realizing that creating affordable housing one property at a time was not a sustainable solution and was straining Wellspring staff. We needed a different model that we could bring our imagination to.

That's when we met Chuck Collins, who was working at the time with the Institute for Community Economics in Greenfield, Massachusetts. Chuck was speaking at an affordable-housing conference about a creative new idea called land trusts, based on the belief that land is a common heritage and housing should be a right. Land and housing should not be commodities. The way it works is a community organization sets up a land trust that buys land and permanently holds it in trust for affordable housing and other community needs. Community members can buy or build homes on the land, with a mortgage lower than they'd pay for rent. The owners get all the legal and tax benefits of home ownership, but they do not own the land. The community land trust does. Owners can sell their homes but not above the purchase price plus any added value from improvements. This protects the land, the residents, and the community from speculation.

We invited Chuck to Wellspring to help the board set up a sister corporation, the Wellspring Community Land Trust of Cape Ann. Our feasibility study showed that including Wellspring's name would give people in town confidence in this new "radical" approach to provide home ownership to low-income families.

As we got to know Chuck better, we learned his personal story and developed a deep friendship that continues to this day. Born in one of the most affluent zip codes in the country, a suburb of Detroit, where he attended private schools with classmates named Iacocca and Romney, Chuck was heir to Oscar Mayer, a German immigrant who founded the hot dog business. In 1967 Chuck witnessed the Detroit riots, when black residents protested police brutality and racial injustice. Seeing the burning buildings and armored tanks of the National Guard, he realized how different his life was from those who were suffering and protesting the injustices in their lives. When he was 16, his father told him that he was going to inherit part of the family fortune as a trust fund. Chuck had mixed reactions. He was grateful, but it didn't seem fair. After high school he did not go immediately to college but to Worcester, Massachusetts, where he worked in a soup kitchen. At age 26, he was working with tenants who were struggling to raise quarters and dollars to buy the land under their mobile homes, when all the while he knew he could just write a check for what they needed. He didn't earn the money, didn't need it, and knew others needed it more. And he wanted to make his own way. So he told his parents he was giving the half a million dollars to organizations he had chosen working for the environment, peace, racial equality, and indigenous and gay people's rights. He wanted to pass on the wealth.

Chuck's father was concerned and flew to meet him the next day. What if Chuck or his future family had some serious illness or accident, and he was the one who had given away the money? Chuck's response was that he'd rather work for a society where people take care of each other and not one where you have to amass a small fortune to provide basic care. Chuck's work with land trusts and mobile home tenants was just the beginning of his life work on affordable housing, income inequality, and a fair economy. Author of several books, he founded the Boston-based United for a Fair Economy (UFE) and now directs the Inequality and the Common Good program at the Institute for Policy Studies based in Washington, DC Chuck and his wife, Mary, now live in Guilford, Vermont, where Chuck continues his work and his writing as well as working the land.

With Chuck's help, the Wellspring Community Land Trust was incorporated in January 1989. Over the next fifteen years it acquired and developed four properties, totaling fifty-one affordable-housing units for people to buy. In 1990 the land trust created the very first permanent affordable house on Cape Ann, a duplex on Taylor Street—a real home, with units that two families would buy and own, not just transitional rooms to rent like the lodging houses we rehabbed.

Then in 1995 the land trust bought a charming 1920s Arts and Crafts brick schoolhouse, the former Forbes Elementary School, from the city for just $1. Architect Tim Thurman was able to keep the high ceilings, huge windows, and even the old blackboards while creating eight units, including two ground-floor handicapped units and two attic units with magnificent views of the city.

The ultimate dream of the land trust was to acquire and transform an entire neighborhood into a healthy place to live, with common space and parking. Between 1992 and 1995 it began acquiring properties on what was then known as Alper Road, Gloucester's most dilapidated, drug-infested, violent "road." We started by creating three units in an abandoned building, which the Essex County Association of the United Church of Christ took on as its mission project. Forty-three congregations raised funds through bake sales, coffeehouses, and bike-a-thons, and hundreds of volunteers helped with demolition (including taking down a three-story chimney, brick by brick), insulation, and painting. In May 1993 the first new owners moved in and immediately planted gardens around their transformed building, reviving the energy of the neighborhood.

Five years later the chance came to make the dream of a whole affordable neighborhood come true. The owners of a big chunk of the area went bankrupt, and the land trust got the first bid to buy. It was a big dream for a small nonprofit and took years of hard work and collaboration to create twenty-seven well-built, energy-efficient, permanently affordable homes, in the New England clapboard style, surrounded by beautiful gardens. We held a contest to choose a new name: Haven Terrace.

Stacy Randell, whom Wellspring hired to direct our family program, bought a condo on Haven Terrace in 1996 and lived there for twenty-five years. At the time she was making $24,000 a year and supporting her 1-year-old child completely on her own. Her childcare costs were $500 a month, more than her mortgage and condo fee combined. Even if she could have found a safe affordable apartment to rent, financial anxiety would have ruled her life, she says. She would not have been able to make ends meet, period. She would have been at the mercy of a landlord who could raise the rent every year, and she would have had to move many times, to potentially unsafe places. She would have had to work multiple jobs and been an absent mother for much of her son's childhood. Because of home ownership, her son grew up in one place, in one neighborhood, with a mom who had time for him. He made lasting friendships that continue to this day. That kind of housing stability during childhood is priceless and is a great contributor to his success now as a man. After graduating five years ago from college, he now has a good scientific job. "Safe affordable housing and support allow every person the opportunity to live rather than simply to survive," Stacy told us. "I am one of those people. My son is one of those people."

***

The last big project took ten years to complete and put great strains on the land trust. In 1993 we acquired two severely dilapidated buildings in an otherwise well-cared-for neighborhood on Granite Street. The ten-unit Victorian row house had once been home to returning Civil War soldiers and later seafarers while their ships were in port. The smaller building had once been a tin factory. At the time of purchase the land trust received lead-free certificates from Gloucester's building department. But copious lead paint was soon discovered in both buildings, requiring us to relocate families during the remediation.

With the costly rehab—much more costly than we had projected—the land trust didn't have enough for its own rent and salaries. Some staff went without salaries, which we argued was foolish. From 1992 to 1995 Wellspring launched a $1 million capital campaign and gave $250,000 to the land trust, but that was quickly used up. Obtaining grants is intensive, time-consuming, endless work. Proposals are very competitive. Even if you are awarded, getting the money can take months, while the organization still must fund its day-to-day operations. And if you don't succeed, you often have to resubmit in the next round. In the affordable-housing world, time is money and adds to project costs. After ten years the land trust sold the condominiums on Granite Street to first-time homebuyers, many of them former renters.

The decade between 2003 and 2013 was difficult for the land trust. There was major inflation in the housing market. Land and properties for affordable development were scarce, and state and federal monies limited. The land trust pared down to only one full-time staff person, the director, and a volunteer board, which eventually and happily decided to merge with Harborlight Community Partners, the North Shore regional affordable-housing nonprofit organization that has developed hundreds of units of rental housing. The fifty-one condos of the Wellspring Land Trust of Cape Ann were its first ownership properties. The land trust still holds title to the land, which ties the resale price to local wage rates, ensuring continued affordability.

***

The land trust definitely helped us have more impact, but we still could never develop affordable housing fast enough to meet the need, which is still growing today. We needed to put more energy into advocating for better housing policy at the local, state, and federal levels. Women living in the shelter, adult learners in our education programs, as well as staff and board members—we all went to Gloucester City Hall, the Massachusetts Statehouse, and the US Capitol. Wellspring sponsored an annual legislative breakfast to meet with state representatives when the state budget was being negotiated. We took our staff, guests, students, tenants, volunteers, donors, and board members to New York City and Washington, DC, for national Housing Now Marches.

Some of us stayed at the large shelter in Washington, DC, founded by Mitch Snyder, the advocate for homeless people. He went on 200 hunger strikes, shaming the Reagan administration and Congress into dealing with the masses of people sleeping on the street, many of them Vietnam veterans. Mitch had spent two years in federal prison, where he had met and was inspired by Philip and Daniel Berrigan, the two priests that had also inspired Father Paul Moritz at St Ann's in Peabody. In the 1980s he and other activists occupied the abandoned Federal City College building, now located at Mitch Snyder Place, welcoming in hundreds of homeless people for the night. Under pressure, the Reagan administration agreed to lease the building to his group, the Community for Creative Non-Violence, for $1. But it was in terrible condition. Mitch fasted nearly to death twice, demanding that the government make the building habitable for the up to 1,000 people sleeping there each night. When a CBS "Sixty Minutes" segment about Mitch's hunger strike aired on the eve of the 1984 election, Reagan capitulated again and promised to make the necessary repairs—a promise he broke.

Mitch visited Wellspring in spring 1990, feeling very low, months before his tragic death by suicide. He walked in the garden and expressed his appreciation for the beauty of the house, the green space, the gardens, and the fragrance of the flower arrangements inside. He was an inspiration and a friend to us.

***

How can we possibly have a just system when such a basic human need—a place to sleep at night, a place to live our lives—is a commodity, rather than a right? On reflection now, we can see we made a mistake in our advocacy work. Housing should be a basic human right. Declaring that right is the first step in solving homelessness. We should have demanded that from both our state and federal governments.

The housing market has been ruthlessly manipulated in our country. It's become an arena to extract wealth from anyone who has to pay rent or a mortgage. It has attracted the worst human instincts for greed, with evil schemes like subprime mortgages, credit default swaps, collateralized debt obligations, and mortgage-backed securities, which have caused so much misery.

The biggest hoop people have to jump through in order to get on board the wealth-building train of home ownership is qualifying for a mortgage—getting together a down payment, a steady income, and a good credit rating. For people who can do that, their home is almost certainly their most valuable asset. With careful budgeting and some luck, they can build a secure financial future around it. But for people at the bottom or even the middle of the income spectrum, qualifying for a mortgage and buying a home can be an impossible hurdle. Home prices are whatever the market can bear, and they usually go up faster than the rest of the economy. There is not enough affordable housing, and there is increasingly extreme income inequality. Lower-income people simply cannot afford to buy a home. That inability has become a wedge that has served to widen our wealth gap over the past century, as well as our racial divide.

Franklin Delano Roosevelt's administration is the only one that truly understood the urgency of making housing a right. In his second inaugural address in 1937 Roosevelt stated: "I see one-third of a nation ill-housed, ill-clad, ill-nourished.... The test of our progress is not whether we add to the abundance of those who have much; it is whether we provide enough for those who have too little." In each of his terms, he worked toward passing that test.

As part of the New Deal, the Federal Housing Administration (FHA) provided funding to help homeowners keep their homes and put construction workers back to work during the Depression. But it did little to help the poorest Americans, especially African Americans.

Three years later the administration funded public housing for the first time, lending hundreds of millions to state and local agencies to construct low-income housing developments. Tenants paid half the rent, and the other half was paid by local, state, or federal governments. The real estate industry fiercely opposed public housing, but in practice the infusion of public money only helped landlords and developers, and it still does.

The 1944 GI Bill of Rights provided World War II veterans with very favorable loan terms and zero down payments, helping build thousands of units of housing in new suburbs. However, again, almost all of this new housing was limited to white applicants.

To help address both wealth and racial inequality, Roosevelt proposed a Second Bill of Rights in his fourth inaugural address, guaranteeing the right of every family to a decent home, as well as jobs, food, education, medical care, and more. He lent his executive staff to key Senate committees to draft a bill, in the hopes of getting it enacted by the end of his fourth term. Sadly, within three months, he was dead.

Vice President Harry Truman, who had met with Roosevelt only twice during their term together, didn't share his passion for the Second Bill of Rights. Truman's priority was ending the war. In his second term he introduced "urban renewal" as his housing policy, which focused on clearing the slums and firetraps out of US cities. In theory, residents would be moved to safer public housing. In reality, tight-knit communities were destroyed, and families and businesses displaced, often with nowhere to go.

Gloucester saw the effects of urban renewal on its waterfront. Lodging houses, homes, apartments, bars, restaurants, and other mom-and-pop businesses were cleared out. Fancy hotels and restaurants went up in their place. Various interests in town fought over the turf: The fishing community wanted continued access to the waterfront. The Chamber of Commerce wanted a tourist center. Historic preservationists wanted to save an iconic five-gabled, granite-block house overlooking the harbor, from which maritime artist Fitz Henry Lane painted his landscapes. Plans and funds for moving were put in place to help the displaced residents and businesses in the waterfront area relocate. But there weren't many places they could afford to move to, nor was there funding to create such places. As one resident who lost housing said, "Where we live now is where we can afford."

Since the 1950s our country has ping-ponged on housing policy, with new administrations undoing what their predecessors had started, then the next one starting over again. President Lyndon Johnson established Housing and Urban Development as a Cabinet-level agency—headed by Robert Weaver, the first African American Cabinet secretary—and enacting the Fair Housing Act, making it illegal to deny housing on the basis of racial or other discrimination, though it is still a common practice.

Jimmy Carter lived his life in the belief that housing should be a human right. After his presidency, he and his wife Rosalynn volunteered with Habitat for Humanity, which has built 70,000 homes and rehabbed 100,000 more, and became its public face. During his single term, though, his administration made little progress on housing policy, needing to focus on the energy crisis, inflation, and a recession.

Then in the 1980s came the devastation of the Reagan administration. Reagan's massive cuts to federal housing funding have never been restored, leaving a legacy of homelessness our country has still not recovered from.

The day Michael Dukakis was inaugurated as Massachusetts governor in 1983, we were at the State House with all our colleagues in the housing advocacy world. We had his attention. He pledged to shelter people without homes and "to fight Reaganomics and its philosophy of indifference with all the energy I can summon." That year he signed what is still the country's only statewide Right to Shelter law, guaranteeing emergency shelter to homeless families and pregnant women. None of us could have foreseen the cost of that policy some forty years later. In just one year the state's emergency family shelter budget jumped 23 percent, to $325 million in 2023, due to rising housing costs, an influx of immigrants and asylum seekers, and the end of pandemic eviction protections.

We learned a tough lesson: Be careful not to ask for too little. We should have demanded *housing* as a right, not just shelter. We should have said for every dollar the state spends on shelter, it must spend a dollar on affordable housing. We can only dream now of how different a world it would be, how much more effectively those dollars would have been spent, and how much less emergency shelter would be needed, if only housing were a right.

Declaring housing as a basic human right does not mean governments should give away houses free of charge to everyone who needs one. But it does create a duty for the government to protect and fulfill that right. That could mean more resources for public housing and vouchers, incentives for developers, more public and private investment in affordable housing, structures to encourage nonprofit and cooperative housing, zoning laws and tax credits, market regulation like rent control, housing codes, and protections from evictions and foreclosures.

Polls show that three-quarters of Americans believe housing should be a human right, according to the National Low-Income Housing Coalition. Countries such as France, South Africa, and Scotland have adopted a right to housing in their constitutions or laws. Scottish law requires local governments to plan for enough affordable-housing stock so that all homeless persons can be immediately housed for as long as needed. Along with a protected right to purchase public housing units and foreclosure prevention programs, these policies work together so that homelessness is rare in Scotland.

Creating affordable housing was challenging, stressful, and expensive, at best. Sometimes it was heartbreaking. But it was also immensely rewarding. Building homes for people was also life giving. It was the very work of justice.

Figure 1:

All of us living together at Wellspring House gathered in front of the huge walk-in hearth on the September day Marygrace McCullough was married in 1984. Standing, left to right, are cofounders Jenny Richards, Rosemary Haughton, Nancy Schwoyer, Paul and Mary Jane Veronese. In the front row are Sissy LaVoie, Mark Baker (who joined us in 1982), and Marygrace. She wore the wedding gown that Rosemary made for her, the only item saved from a fire in our room, the whole day.

Figure 2: Our first guest, Ellen Kelly, arrived on December 8, 1981, traumatized after a fire destroyed the building where she had a room in exchange for running errands for an elderly man. Raised in foster care since birth, she moved into an apartment in our first affordable-housing venture four years later, giving her the comfort and security of her own place for the first time in her life.

Figure 3: Between 1983 and 1987 Shirley and Ron, a couple who had met and spent years at a state mental-health hospital, were our weekend guests, sleeping on the foldout couch on the sunporch. In the 1980s institutions across the country began discharging patients into "community care," often with no more than $20 in their pockets. But the community-living services envisioned by the advocates of deinstitutionalization largely did not exist yet. People with mental disabilities and challenges often ended up on the streets.

Figure 4: Board member Barbara Simpson was a powerhouse. Growing up poor and orphaned, she got an engineering degree and ran her own successful cabinetmaking business. Jumping on a chair at a board meeting in the early 1990s, Barbara inspired us to launch a $1 million capital campaign for a new education center and other needs, despite a down economy and two other big capital campaigns going on in town.

Figure 5: From the moment Ann Louise Gilligan and Katherine Zappone spontaneously showed up at the Wellspring House door our first year, they became our dearest friends and soul mates in our shared mission of empowering women to break the cycle of poverty. Influenced by Wellspring House, they founded An Cosán, a sister organization outside Dublin, Ireland, that provided education for women in poverty. When we started our education center, we invited them to be our first Scholars in Residence. In May 1996 we raised a glass in gratitude for all we had learned from them.

Figure 6: Lena Novello (right), president of the Gloucester Fishermen's Wives Association, teaches Wellspring cofounder Sissy LaVoie (left) and development director Paula Flynn how to clean and cook underutilized fish in Wellspring's Fish to People program in the late 1990s. Lena, a formidable and respected presence in the city, argued at endless meetings and hearings against the federal regulations that decimated family fishing businesses in Gloucester.

Figure 7: In June 2007 Wellspring House board members, staff, and volunteers celebrated Rosemary Haughton (center, in red jacket), on her retirement as associate director and clerk, though she continued to care for her beloved gardens. At her sides are Wellspring cofounders Mary Jane Veronese and Nancy Schwoyer. Planning for Nancy's retirement as executive director the following year, the board was clear that they did not want the kind of transition where the outgoing director clears her desk and disappears.

CHAPTER 7

Celebration

Celebration is one of the things that distinguishes us as human beings. It brings a community together. Celebration draws on a well of emotional and spiritual energy from past times and encourages us for the future. To celebrate is to seize a moment of life that has power, such as the birth of a new baby or the liberation of a nation.

At Wellspring House, we believed that weaving large and small celebrations into our life together as a community was essential, week in, week out, through hard times as well as good. It was a big difference between Wellspring House and other shelters, nonprofits, and social-service agencies. Taking time to observe birthdays and graduations and many other events in the lives of families in the shelter injected joy and hope into the weeks of waiting, filling out forms, and making trips to the welfare office.

The birthday girl or boy always got to choose the menu for the fifteen to twenty people at dinner: pizza, spaghetti, ice cream cake, or even better, Mom's chocolate cake. The kids also loved the macaroni and cheese and shepherd's pie Rosemary made from scratch. On the moms' birthdays, the women often asked to cook their own favorite meal: perhaps beans and rice and plantains. At first that sounded a little plain to us non-Latinas, but it was so good everyone begged for it, topped off with the hot sauce Nancy bought, which our guests never thought was hot enough. Nancy did the shopping every Saturday, making sure to put any special celebration food on her list. After Nancy became executive director, staff and volunteers would often say, "I can't believe you're still doing that." Nancy would reply, "It's the only thing I feel I can finish!" On Paul's birthday, we always ordered a chocolate-covered donut the size of a dinner plate.

When a family got a new home, we held a leaving party and sent them off with a laundry basket filled with donated household goods, in which brushes and detergents almost acquired a certain glamor. Those parties also cheered the families still waiting, giving them hope their turn would come.

Every Saturday night we gathered before dinner to give thanks for the week that had just passed, sharing with one another whatever disappointments or good news it had held, and to share our hopes for the week to come. Rosemary had adapted prayers that we said to welcome in the Sabbath, and she made little flat loaves we ate with wine or juice. One of the mothers lit the candles in the replica eighteenth-century chandelier hanging over the table. The kids loved sharing about their week—that they got new sneakers, or went to the beach, or saw Daddy—and they loved having the floor with everyone listening to them. Their mothers often tried to get them to wrap it up more quickly. Some families continued the ritual when they were in their own homes.

We believed in infusing beauty, attention, and meaning into each of those moments, whether rites of passage, traditional holidays, or celebrations we invented ourselves. We found ways to make what we had special, without spending a lot: food, flowers, candles, singing, dancing, and our own creativity and heartfelt expressions to one another. We didn't look at celebration as just fun or nice to do. It was essential for the families who came to us—actually, for all of us—and for the social change we sought in the world.

***

Our guests and their children loved to celebrate Christmas, for the most part. But just as Christmas can be beautiful and moving, it can also be stressful and painful, especially for people with no home. It took us a while to figure out how to navigate our own giving instincts at Christmastime—and how to celebrate the holiday sensitively so that our gifts and gestures could be received with the joy we hoped for. It's a lesson all of American culture could learn.

For the four weeks leading up to Christmas, the children took turns each evening opening the little doors on our Advent calendar. On Saturday evening we lit one more of the four Advent candles, purple ones for hope, love, and peace and a pink one for joy, which were set in an evergreen wreath on the chandelier.

Rosemary always made a traditional English Christmas pudding on the first Sunday of Advent, known in England as "Stir Up Sunday" from the Anglican prayer "Stir up, O Lord, the hearts of thy faithful people." She mixed enormous quantities of dried fruit, flour, suet, dark brown sugar, and spices. Then everyone in the house took a turn stirring it up in a big pudding bowl. Each stirrer got to make a wish, though many of our guests didn't know what they were stirring—and wouldn't touch it when the time came to eat it weeks later (even some of Rosemary's family won't eat it). But we all loved the ritual. At the end of our Christmas feast Rosemary turned the dark concoction out on a plate, poured brandy over it, lit it with a hovering blue flame, carried it to the darkened sunporch, and served it to the more adventurous eaters with an English hard sauce of butter and sugar, while we all sang, "Good tidings we bring to you and your kin. We wish you a Merry Christmas and a Happy New Year."

Before Christmas the smells of pies baking and of turkey roasting filled the old house. On Christmas Eve anyone who wished would gather in the chapel, where we read the Christmas story, shared our reflections, and sang carols. We always had a tree up to the ceiling in the sunporch, flashing with lights and baubles, and gifts under it.

It was the gifts—and the extreme excess around Christmas in America—that were the most problematic part of the holiday. And it took us a while to get that right.

Christmas is a time when many people think of those who are poor. Some are also moved to give to charity before the end of the tax year. Sometimes those who have just give and give to those who do not have. That can feel humiliating to parents who already resent the dependence of being homeless or poor. It can make them feel even more invisible, as though giving gifts at Christmas is enough attention, and it's fine to ignore the needs of people who are poor on all the other days. One mother told us, "Christmas has to be more than one day in the year." Our guests did not want charity. They wanted a way to lift themselves out of a system that made it nearly impossible for them to provide enough for their children.

One year donors labeled their wrapped presents for the intended recipient, say, for a boy age 4, or for a girl size six. We couldn't allow that. It's hard to think of anything that would make someone feel more invisible than a gift, from an anonymous giver, for an anonymous recipient. We quickly changed those labels to the children's names before the parents ever saw the gifts.

Another year some of our donors asked our guests to make a dream list. One little boy in a booster chair on Christmas morning, loaded with presents, put his head down and whimpered, "It's too much, Mommy, too much." His mom told us later, "I cannot do this next year." That was something we often heard from our guests about the extravagance of Christmas.

Sometimes families in the community wanted to drop off used stuffed animals to make room for the new ones their own kids would be getting on Christmas Day. We handed the toys back and politely let them know: "The children at Wellspring House will all get new toys."

Or some parents wanted *their* kids to have the experience of giving gifts to children who were poor, children they didn't know. Again, we told them politely, "No, thank you."

The mothers at Wellspring House wanted something special for their children at Christmas. They appreciated the goodwill of others. But *they* wanted to choose and give their kids gifts. They didn't want us to do it. They certainly didn't want strangers doing it.

What Wellspring eventually settled on—an idea we got from Project Hope in Boston's Roxbury neighborhood—was a "holiday store" on a weekend in mid-December. The two weeks after Thanksgiving donors brought unwrapped new gifts, for babies to teens, but no violent toys, not even water pistols. They also brought items that children could give their mothers, like cosmetics, scarves, jewelry, and stationery. For 50 cents or $1, parents who participated in any of Wellspring's programs could choose their own gifts to give to their children, which included a roll of wrapping paper. Each child also received a book from the store. While their mothers shopped, the children could make cards, do puzzles, and go with a volunteer to pick out and wrap a gift for their mothers. Many were so excited, they'd say, "Open it now!" Wellspring House also put our own gift—usually a sweater, each one different, personally selected by a staff member in a style, size, and color with each mother in mind—under the tree on the sunporch.

If our guests had family nearby, we encouraged them to spend Christmas Day together if possible. But that was not always a happy time. Families in shelter found it hard to be visitors in other people's homes when they had no home. For some, family relationships were strained and painful. They often came back to Wellspring after only one night. For whoever was in the house on Christmas Day, we always had a big traditional dinner. Founders and old friends always joined if they were in the area.

If we had guests who didn't celebrate Christmas, we tried to welcome and celebrate with them, too. One year we bought a little menorah and candles for a Jewish mother and child who were our guests. For eight nights we celebrated Hanukkah, learned the special prayers and songs, and told the story of the Maccabees and the rededication of the Temples with a lamp that never went out during the days of the feast.

***

At Wellspring, we also celebrated Passover alongside Easter in the spring, and it became our most meaningful celebration of our year. Rosemary grew up with family on her immigrant grandmother's side who were all proud of their Jewish heritage. She had begun celebrating Passover with her own family when her older children were teenagers. All of us at our parish in Peabody, especially Marygrace and Nancy, had helped put on a modified Passover feast, the Seder, to observe the story of the Exodus, when Moses liberated the Jewish people enslaved by the Egyptian Pharoah.

The Hebrew scripture message of social justice and freedom from oppressors resonated with all of us at Wellspring. Our community of founders identified with the people of Israel, leaving our settled lives to go into a new land, not knowing what challenges and risks we would face. The symbol was resonant, too, for families in shelter who had been driven from their homes into the modern-day wilderness and for whom the promised land seemed very far off. In our society women who are homeless are the lowest of all and live in a kind of slavery. The underlying assumptions that once allowed women to be the property of men have not changed very much, even though laws about women's rights to property, custody of children, and rights to their own earnings have. The fact of a person's being homeless is the expression of society's judgment that a person lacks humanity. Once someone has failed to hold onto property, whether a home or a job, that person is dependent on others' decisions. She is expected to accept rudeness, wait in line, be grateful, and respond to the demands of those in power. She is still "spiritually" the property of others. Coming to that understanding is what made our Passover celebration so powerful.

Every spring we ironed the tablecloths—or white sheets if we didn't have enough—and got out our best dishes. Early on, when our budget was tight, we actually had a community meeting to decide whether we could afford to buy a nice tablecloth and napkins for our Seder table. We decided yes, we could and should. Rosemary rolled out dough into paper-thin sheets and baked matzahs with no yeast or leavening, to remember how quickly the Jewish people had to flee their homes, with no time for their daily bread to rise. We dipped watercress as a symbol of the bitterness of slavery into bowls of saltwater representing tears. When evening came, we blessed the candles and wine and took turns round the table reading the prayers. The youngest present asked the ancient question: "Why is this night different from all other nights?" At the end, like Jews around the world going back millennia, we called out: "Next year in Jerusalem!" For our Wellspring guests, we added: "Next year in my own home!"

Passover usually fell in the same week as Easter, a Christian celebration with roots in millennia-old pagan festivals of new life emerging from the darkness of winter. We loved celebrating both holidays of spring and fertility. On Easter morning the children at Wellspring took little baskets to hunt for eggs in the gardens and bushes, as the women in Jerusalem went looking for a dead Jesus and met a living one. Paul, who loved chocolate so much, always went on the hunt, too.

The night before, we started a fire with some dry twigs in an old galvanized-steel washtub out in the yard and lit our big paschal candle. From there we passed the flame to smaller candles we each held and carried the light into the darkened house. Most of our women guests came to this ritual. We had prepared the house by taking away all the old candles, putting out fresh linens, and filling the rooms with flowers. Then we brought the paschal light to the new candles in each room and finally the chapel. There, we blessed a bowl of water, then blessed one another, and read and sang the story of the power of life breaking through death.

One Easter everyone at Wellspring experienced that power in a way we will never forget. Some years earlier a young woman, Linda, had come to the shelter with her little boy. She'd had a hard life, struggling with addiction, which she finally overcame. She was able to move to a new home and a job. But shortly after moving into her own place, just in her 30s, she was diagnosed with breast cancer, and it had metastasized. As the disease progressed, her son was placed in foster care. Linda was admitted to Gloucester's Addison Gilbert Hospital and was about to be moved to hospice care on the same campus. The hospital social worker happened to be Kathy McIntyre, who was Wellspring's first board president.

"I don't want to go there to die," Linda told Kathy.

"What do you want?" Kathy asked.

"I want to go home. I want to go back to Wellspring House. Do you think that's possible?"

Kathy picked up the phone and called Nancy, who replied, "It's absolutely possible."

It was Easter weekend. We brought a hospital bed into a ground-floor room known as the study. On Saturday morning an ambulance brought Linda and a nurse to Wellspring. We weren't preparing for someone to die. We were preparing to be with her. Our Easter celebrations continued in other rooms and the yard, but in that quiet room, filled with candles and gentle music, people came and went, to just sit with her.

Then it was Easter morning. Outside could be heard the joyful voices of children hunting for eggs. One of them was Linda's son, whose foster parents had brought him over to spend the day. What was most on her mind was her son's future. We arranged for our friend, attorney Rick Porter, to bring Linda papers that allowed his foster parents, whom she knew loved him, to adopt. Once she signed the papers, she drifted in and out of sleep, only rousing when her child came to sit on her bed and hug her, then ran off to play with the other children. Elsewhere in the house Easter dinner was celebrated, but it did not disturb the peace and beauty of the room where Linda lay. Toward evening her boy came and kissed her one last time, and she died. That was an extraordinary space and time to experience the closeness of life and death. Her memorial service was at Wellspring, and her young son welcomed and thanked people for coming. Linda finally got what she wanted and needed. She was home, she was accepted and loved, and she knew her little boy would be taken care of.

***

There was one other celebration in the Wellspring calendar that was especially beloved by all the women at Wellspring—founders, staff, volunteers, board members, shelter guests, and friends—a women-only ritual that we all created together. Each December we observed the winter solstice to experience the longest night of the year. We started in the living room, lit a warming fire in the fireplace, and read Rosemary's poem "Darkest Night":

> It is time for incantation, time to enter
> The narrow passage to the sacred place.
> At the centre. Blade of midwinter sheaths
> Into the birthing chamber; it is time to run
> With the wise women, the midwife crones,
> Into the dark, round inner space, chanting the tones
> Of our ancient call, women of skill,
> Coming out of time past to fulfill the present.
> Lead us unto the birthplace, the time is near.
> In the heart of the earth the year waits
> For the women's hands to receive the newborn Sun.

Next we lit candles while singing the carol "The Holly and the Ivy," and filed into the darkened chapel, taking our places on cushions or chairs in a circle. In the middle was a big bowl of water, the same bowl we used to make bread, circled by evergreen branches. A flat rock in the bowl held a small candle we called the moon candle. In the room lit only by our small candle flames there was a deep sense of community and trust as all reflected silently on the experience of darkness in the year that was ebbing.

Those who wished would name the darkness in their lives—events, fears, disappointments, tragedies, whether public or personal. These were not women who knew each other intimately, but the space created an intimacy where we could sometimes give voice to pain we had kept hidden. One woman shared that her brother had committed suicide. Another discovered her son was gay, which broke her heart, not that he was gay, but that he didn't feel he could share that with her. Another grieved for the polar bears and the melting Arctic.

Once everyone had spoken, one at a time, each woman gently blew out her candle. Last we extinguished the moon candle and sat with the darkness for a while, until someone softly started a chant that swelled: "The seasons turn. We bring the light. We call the sun from the dark night."

Then we set a big fat golden candle on the rock, relit our candles, poured rosewater and golden glitter in the water, and splashed each other's faces with the sparkly scented water, which lingered on us all for days. We sang and danced in a circle around the candle, then outside to the patio where we lit a fire in the same steel washtub we used at Easter. One year Wellspring volunteer Jane Saltonstall folded her long kilt up and leaped right over the fire. Then we howled at the moon. Sometimes neighborhood dogs howled back. At first, only a few women came to our solstice celebration. But the number steadily grew, and we adapted and changed our observance over the years. Clearly, a ritual observing darkness and celebrating the return of the light met a need.

***

Like all nonprofits, we held many fund-raisers over the years. They were necessary, but we also tried to make them celebratory. Over and over we were overwhelmed with gratitude at how all Cape Ann turned out to donate time, talent, use of beautiful homes and event spaces, and money, making clear that Wellspring was an important part of community life.

For "Broadway under the Stars" in 1996, electricians laid yards of light and sound cables; printers donated posters, tickets, and programs; and local actors, dancers, and musicians performed excerpts from Broadway shows, against a background of flowering shrubs and trees as night fell.

Tickets for "The Big Night," celebrating Wellspring's twentieth anniversary in 2001, included dinner provided by seventeen local families in their own homes, followed by a parody show called "The Beat Goes On" written and directed for us by Richard Earle in Stage Fort Park.

The most memorable was "On the Waterfront," held in the huge loading bay of the Americold fish-packing company. Americold employees were so supportive of the event, they contacted freighters far at sea to make sure they didn't arrive to be unloaded at the dock during the event. The workers scrubbed and whitewashed the whole place and cleaned up one of the gents' staff restrooms (including the graffiti) for women. From a walkway along the harbor, guests were greeted by a rainbow-hued arch of water from a fire service boat, before making their way to a harborside dinner, a documentary about Wellspring directed by local filmmaker Henry Ferrini, and a vaudeville show. The finale was a male striptease inspired by the movie *The Full Monty*. Men in full fishermen's gear of yellow slickers, sou'westers, and seaboots danced and gradually shed it all. In the final moment, to roars and cheers, what was revealed was a large red plastic lobster in the appropriate place.

After our twentieth anniversary our board felt we needed to bring the Wellspring House story into Boston. We needed more space for our fundraisers, and we needed to reach out to people in government, finance, and industry in all of Massachusetts. We booked a date at the Boston Center for the Arts, a spectacular circular space with a brick floor, copper dome, and skylight called the Cyclorama, which was built in 1884 to house a panoramic painting of "The Battle of Gettysburg." One of our speakers, Kathy Martinez, told how her husband was unjustly deported and she was left homeless with three daughters. She saw a Wellspring flyer at a street fair and got accepted in our education programs, where she found support. Wellspring changed her life, and she was now in law school.

When she finished, our emcee, New England Patriots football legend Tedy Bruschi, leaped onto the stage to a roar of applause and put his arm around her shoulder. "My wife and I were talking last night," he told her. "I can't imagine what it's like to be homeless. Then I met you and heard your story." He picked up one of the beautiful orbs that were on each table, made by potter Miranda Thomas. Inspired by Wellspring's logo, painted limbs and leaves elegantly twisted around each black-glazed pottery globe. On the tree a healed scar marked where a branch had broken. Miranda provided this artist note: "The tree of life since ancient times has been the symbol of shelter and the enrichment of life, its branches reaching outwards, growing, leafing out and blooming into infinity. I always include on the trunk of the tree a healed broken branch. This symbolizes the struggle and pains of growing and the ultimate healing and moving forward. The spring of knowledge flows beneath and feeds the tree." Tedy announced to the crowd of more than 300 people: My wife and I are going to start the bidding at $2,000 for this orb on our table, and I invite the rest of you to do the same." That night we more than tripled what we had ever raised before.

CHAPTER 8

What Is Radical Hospitality?

"What you were doing was *radical* hospitality!" Soon after we retired as directors of Wellspring House in 2008, a group of "alums" began to meet every few weeks for a meal in one of our homes. At one of those reunions, folks made this remark.

That took us aback. It never felt that way at the time. It felt natural to how we had lived our lives as a community, our principles, our faith, and how we wanted to be in the world. Reflecting on it now, we see that Wellspring House was, indeed, radical.

Our bedrock principle of mutuality. The way we celebrated with our guests. Our disciplined democratic process. Our inspiration from Freire's theory of education as the key to the transformation of poverty. The inclusion of founders, staff, board, and guests in most of what we did, including evaluations and strategic planning, as well as meals and cleaning. All of these were radical in the world of nonprofits and social services.

When we first started, our hospitality idea seemed simple: we wanted to share our lives with one another and with people who needed a home for a while. But we soon discovered that meant welcoming people and ideas strange to us, and that challenged and changed us. That's where the radical part came in. We found ourselves in the vanguard of movements addressing sexism, poverty, housing, and how they intersected. We confronted the way the world saw and treated women, people who were poor, and people without homes.

Many nonprofits choose to do one thing well, get better and better at it, and grow bigger. That wasn't us. We wanted social change. Most of the world operated on the assumption that people who were poor needed rehabilitation—mental-health services, incentives to work and to better their lives, along with the constant advice and criticism that went with that assumption. What needed rehabilitating, we believed, was an economic system that was organized to keep them poor. As one guest told us, "I'm not a lost cause. I think the world has to change, not me personally."

People who don't have enough money are too often acted upon, unconsulted, assumed to be unable to make their own future. We believed in listening to the people we were serving. We learned from them. And we went outside our comfort zone to try things we had no experience in, such as developing affordable housing. We had rules and agreements, but we rejected the hierarchical structures of most nonprofits and agencies. We, of course, observed boundaries, but they weren't rigid. In our commitment to create an interdependent community, and also to make our connections more human, we stretched those boundaries between helper-helped, teacher-learner, employee-boss, professional-volunteer, and workmate-friend.

We now realize that our not seeing more clearly just how radical we were may have contributed to what happened when it came time for us to step down and pass the baton of leadership on.

***

In 1987 two old friends of Nancy's from St Mary-of-the-Woods College in Indiana, Sister Jeanne Knoerle and Tracy Schier, rang to see if she'd like to have lunch in Rockport, where they were spending a few days. Nancy and Tracy had become friends as students working toward their bachelor's degrees in communication arts together. Jeanne had been the chair of the department, then later college president and chancellor. Now she was retired, and she and Tracy had just created a firm called Woods Associates to assist nonprofit groups like ours with strategies, planning, management, and marketing.

We'd always had a vision of social change through the practice of hospitality. But we had never done much organizational development work. Our organization was growing. We had ten staff people. We thought the first thing we needed was a five-year strategic plan. Jeanne and Tracy persuaded us to start with a mission statement. All sorts of people—potential grant funders, donors, community partners, state and local agencies, job interviewees, volunteers—kept asking all of us what we were and why we were doing what we did. Every day we felt the need for a clear and compelling mission statement that everyone involved with Wellspring could understand and embrace.

Jeanne and Tracy said they'd help us. Fortunately, we had funds to pay them. Ruth McCambridge, the new director of the Fund for the Homeless, had visited us and offered to help fund the organizational work we needed to do. The mission statement we came up with still feels radical, but it wasn't easy getting there.

We gathered the strategic planning committee—board members, staff, and volunteers—eighteen of us, around tables in the chapel. We all agreed that Wellspring was a community. But when Tracy asked, "What kind of community?" we found ourselves arguing about religion, the very thing that had brought us together.

Mary Jane recalled the letter the founders had written in our first weeks in the house to let friends know what we were doing: "We are a group of Christian people ... who have bought a house in which we will live in community ... to be a place of hospitality for people in trouble."

Mark Baker, who was now board chair, had not been part of Wellspring at its founding. An Episcopal priest, he was attracted to Wellspring as a place where he could live out his Christian faith but in a freer and less churchy way. "I believe we need to claim where our commitment comes from," he said in his big baritone voice, which was both convinced and convincing.

Some had been drawn to Wellspring because they wanted to work for justice and do something practical to make real change. Some were deeply religious, like Mark, but expressed it in different ways. Elizabeth Sternberg had come into our lives when she helped us with the development of the Washington Street house and was now on our board. She agreed with Mark about commitment: "For me, the thing that attracted me to Wellspring as a Jew was that it was driven by its religious ethic. We need to own who we are."

This was a difficult part of our conversation, for a while teetering on disagreement. Yet the seemingly contradictory expressions all came out of passion and compassion, and the sense that we were part of a real and exciting newness. Some suggested phrases like "Judeo-Christian" and "faith-based" as compromises.

"Why can't we own who we are?" Mark begged.

Annie Thomas, our volunteer coordinator, was new to Wellspring and had grown up as the daughter of a prominent Unitarian Universalist minister. She remembers being awestruck by the scope of thought being explored in the room and grateful that others wanted to hear *her* thoughts. "What attracted me was seeing the founders walking the walk of social justice, not just talking the talk." she said. "This isn't limited to church traditions, however familiar or precious. We need to be clear that our mission statement is a shared vision, not inherited beliefs."

It was Mary Jane who squared the circle. "It's about faith." she said simply. She didn't mean a belief. "It's about what makes us want to do what we do."

Rosemary added, "It's essentially inclusive. We are interdependent."

Annie's and Rosemary's words reminded us of the women who came to us and changed us. So many of them had been hurt by religious language that was blaming and punishing. Many had rejected organized religion. We heard it over and over: "What have I done that God is punishing me? I must have done something terribly wrong." Many believed that their homelessness was God's punishment and God's will.

We did not want to use language in our mission statement that implied that anyone at Wellspring had to be believers in some religion in order to be acceptable. We wanted to welcome people who believed anything or nothing, creating an atmosphere where people could pursue issues that mattered to them and express their feelings.

During this whole discussion Jeanne and Tracy accompanied us. Most nonprofit organizations use a mission statement to describe the work they do or aspire to do. We wanted a statement that made clear *why* we were doing that work. We agreed not to use phrases like "faith-based" or "Judeo-Christian." But we would use *faith,* as in "a community of faith." Once we reached that consensus. Annie remembers feeling such joy in the room. After years of working together, we knew that our faith was *in one another*. Just saying that was energizing to us.

Our mission statement came together quickly, the words tumbling out:

Wellspring is a community of faith,
aware that each life touches every other life.
Our work and our decisions are therefore
guided by the vision of a just society
in which we must care for the earth and her people
by using our resources, property and land
in a spirit of hospitality.
In this spirit we work to meet basic human needs,
and participate in social change through the provision
of shelter, affordable housing, local economic opportunity and education
rooted in community needs.

For more than twenty years we would keep that short text in our hearts and minds as we carried out the work to which it committed us, everything from taking out the kitchen compost bucket to stretching to meet all the human needs that confronted us. Our framed mission statement stood on each staff member's desk. We read it aloud before all our meetings, weekly staff meetings, board meetings, planning meetings. If someone presented an idea, we always asked: Does it fit what we said in the mission statement? It was front and center in every decision that Wellspring made.

***

Today we are heartened when we hear so many nonprofit, social-service, and advocacy organizations make commitments to "center frontline communities." That means the people who are suffering because of unjust systems hold their own answers. They should be asked what to do. They should be listened to. And they should lead the movements working on social change.

That was exactly the ideal Wellspring aspired to from our beginnings in the early 1980s. It by no means originated with us. We were following the model developed by Paulo Freire, author of *Pedagogy of the Oppressed*, whom Nancy studied with when she was getting her master's in theology and education. One of the Freirean principles we practiced was Action/Reflection, also known as *praxis*.

Every step of the way, as our staff grew, as we added programs, we were stopping to reflect on the actions we had taken. Every week we met with the staff and asked: How has the week gone? What went well? What didn't? How have we advanced the mission? Where have we not done that? What do we need to do, next week but also going forward from there?

Nicole Richon-Schoel, who started as a case manager and later became Wellspring's family life advocate, reminded us of an incident she brought to one of those staff meetings. While working one weekend, she passed a guest in the dark, narrow upstairs hallway. Something about the woman's appearance or maybe it was body language just didn't feel right. She thought that she might be using alcohol or drugs. One of Wellspring's rules was no alcohol or substance abuse. Nicole, who had started at Wellspring as a secretary transcribing Rosemary's handwritten notes, had no social-work training. She knew she had to say something. The two women were very close in the hall. "The guest was tough and street smart. I was not," Nicole remembers.

Terrified, Nicole took a big breath. "Have you been using drugs or alcohol? Are you high?" The guest drew even closer, nose to nose, swore at Nicole, then turned into her room where her three children were watching, and slammed the door. Wellspring had protocols about handling such situations: let people cool down, then make an overture, review the rules, come to an agreement and resolve the issue before the next staff person came on shift. We all followed those protocols so many times they became routine and unremarkable.

What stayed in Nicole's memory of her first such confrontation was the following staff meeting. She recounted what had happened to her new colleagues. She was anxious that she had not handled the situation well. Nancy assured her that doubt and fear were inevitable. The staff expressed their appreciation that she had the courage to speak up and how important that was for the safety of everyone at Wellspring.

"This was like nothing I had ever experienced," Nicole recalls. "I started to understand what a long learning curve I had embarked on. I was called on to take risks, to recognize the divisions between people with courage and compassion, and always to extend my hand as a bridge. My colleagues would always support me. In other work settings, you never get that feeling: We are all there with you in what happened in the hallway."

That kind of reflection went on week in, week out. Often the staff needed to talk at those meetings about what had been hard or stressful that week. There was a whole range of emotions that went with serving guests who had led such hard lives and the nitty-gritty of people living together and sharing a kitchen, bathrooms, and common spaces. We reviewed how the guests' housing searches were going, how their children were doing, were they getting social services they needed, did they need resources for domestic violence or addictions, what steps had been made to get them into permanent housing, and were landlords getting back to us?

The meetings were full of energy and typically lasted an hour and a half. Staff members also brought to the group mistakes they had made. Like Nicole, very few of our hires had social-work backgrounds. Starting with ourselves as founders, we were all constantly learning on the job. Sometimes staff proposed new ideas about how we could serve our guests and our mission better. We had quickly learned that shelters were a very temporary solution to homelessness. Our guests needed so much more: affordable housing, good-paying jobs, more education, childcare, access to better nutrition, legal help, and protection from domestic violence were just a few. We were constantly considering ideas about how our little organization could have more impact.

We brought Action/Reflection into all our meetings, for our various committees, the board, the meetings we required guests to attend to address their housing searches and other needs. Every five years we held a forum and invited our board, volunteers, community members, guests, and students—anyone who had a stake in Wellspring. Again, we asked: What did we do well? What did we miss? How can we better meet the needs of our community? How can we make Gloucester a more sustainable community? It was a discipline. Other organizations sometimes came to our forums just to observe and learn the process.

***

After drafting the mission statement, we turned to making a strategic plan and set five goals for the next five years. One of the goals excited us *far* more than the others. Because of Wellspring's belief that celebrating all together in a community was almost as essential as housing, food, and clothing, we knew one party would not be enough for our tenth anniversary in 1991. We wanted to celebrate the whole year!

We hired Annie Thomas to organize months of celebrations leading up to an evening gala on August 3, the date we had closed on 302 Essex Avenue. Annie, who later became our development director, had such a gift for bringing volunteers together harmoniously, no small feat. People always said, "I love to work at Wellspring events. There's never any fighting. It's so fun." The calendar was packed with luncheons, dinners, teas, parties, talks, and fireside chats around the big hearth of the eighteenth-century house with local leaders about public issues. The central event was a symposium at the end of May, gathering former shelter guests, staff, volunteers, board, as well as bankers, teachers, health professionals, builders, fishermen from Cape Ann, many of whom would never have met otherwise.

While visiting Rosemary's family in England the previous Christmas, we had checked out a folk singer, Janet Russell, at the Black Swan pub in York, and were captivated by her warm alto, humorous patter, and at-times rageful songs about the plight of women. Like real groupies, we chatted her up after the concert and found ourselves inviting her to Massachusetts. We staged her concert at the Episcopal church in Gloucester at a celebration in July. Actress Roberta Nobleman gave a series of one-woman plays during the year, one about the fourteenth-century mystic Julian of Norwich, the first woman to write a book in English, *The Revelations of Divine Love*, which was re-discovered and become a best-seller.

It was a fun year.

***

Mutuality was another practice we were committed to, and it too was a radical difference from other organizations working on poverty, especially at that time. Today mutuality has almost become jargon in social-service circles. It's closely related to "centering frontline communities" and "justice, diversity, equity, and inclusion" but more. It can be hard to define—and we would be the first to say—very hard for both organizations and individuals to live up to.

Mutuality is the belief that, no matter what our roles or circumstances at any moment, we are all in community with one another. It is breaking down the barriers between "us" and "them," between the people who have housing, jobs, and power and those who do not. It is not letting an institution stand in the way of being human with one another.

Mutuality is a belief in generosity, hospitality, and reciprocity. We are all in need of help and able to provide help at different times in our lives.

We are each a human being with huge capacities and challenges, whether we're rich or poor, young or old, more or less educated, have more or fewer abilities. In every relationship, sometimes we are the teachers, sometimes the learners.

Each of us deserves to be listened to, and has the obligation to listen to others, because each of us is the expert on our own life and experiences. That mutual listening is essential to making good decisions and finding good solutions together.

We've already mentioned some examples of practicing mutuality: How we decided to pay taxes to our larger community, the city of Gloucester, rather than seek a nonprofit exemption; we provided a service, and we wanted to pay for our share of services received. How in our earliest days we decided that we founders were a community of equals and would all share in decision making as well as the work, something the construction workers we hired to renovate the house found confounding. How we persuaded Ernie that we really wanted him to come back to the lodging house after it was renovated and homey—he was the reason we were doing it, and he was equally worthy as anyone else. How everyone in the shelter shared in the ordinary tasks of making it a home, taking turns cooking, doing dishes, taking out the compost, and working weekends, including helping guests clean the house on Saturdays. Rosemary usually cleaned the living room, and Nancy did the food shopping. We did not ask the guests to do anything we would not do ourselves.

One of our favorite stories about mutuality involves our first guest, Ellen. Even after Mary Jane moved with Paul to their own Cape-style house, she continued to be Ellen's representative payee, driving her to the bank and errands and helping her budget. In the mid-1990s Mary Jane was diagnosed with macular degeneration and eventually lost most of her vision. She asked Ellen to come over. She told her she couldn't drive her anymore. Ellen now had a home and a car, an old Pontiac she called Mister Sister. She was so proud of that car. Without missing a beat, she informed Mary Jane that she would be driving her now, laughing and laughing: "I never thought the day would come when I would cart *your* ass around Gloucester!"

Mary Lewis, a family life advocate and case manager at Wellspring, wrote a reflection about mutuality in the book *Parenting in Public* by Donna Haig Friedman. One mother constantly took cookies and milk up to her room in the evenings. This was against the rules because of concerns about rodent and insect infestations in an old house where so many people lived together. It was actually a rule from the Gloucester Health Department, which periodically showed up unannounced to inspect the kitchen and the bedrooms for crumbs and dirty glasses. She knew the rule, and she had been spoken to about breaking it. Yet she continued to do it.

Homeless families have gone through a great deal of loss, criticism, and shame, Mary wrote. For many, their belief that they are "good enough" parents is the one thing they have left. So in her interactions with guests, Mary strove to *ask* rather than direct, *listen* rather than assume, and *respect* rather than judge.

She started by asking what sharing evening cookies and milk meant to their family. The mother told her it was a family ritual. They got to spend some nurturing time together, and she could help her children prepare for the next day. Her daughter was having a difficult adjustment to the shelter, strange new people, and a new school. They brainstormed a list of other ways the mother had nurtured the family and some new ones she might try—ways that were acceptable in the shelter community, such as extra-special treats at snack time or games their family had invented and could play together in the playroom. And Mary relearned the lesson that in her job, she needed to restrain her instinct to discipline or give advice and to consider parenting strategies she hadn't thought of.

"Mutuality in a relationship meant that both the mother and I are affecting each other and being affected by each other," Mary wrote. "I am open to the influence that she brings. I am no longer expert and mother to the client; rather, I am a partner in her effort to find and establish the goals that she has for her family. This mutuality helps to lessen the familiar power dynamics that often separate people."

***

Another of the five goals in our strategic plan was to evaluate what we had done so far, to take a hard look at what had succeeded and what had not. This turned out to be the ultimate practice of mutuality. Many organizations would hire an outside research firm to come in and give their opinion on what they saw. We didn't want that. We said to our guests and former guests: You are the experts. You tell us how we're doing and what we need to do. And we'll act on it. We wanted to hear their voices directly.

With the help of an anonymous donation, we hired Helen Hemminger, who had experience with Participative Action Research (PAR), in which the researcher does not view the subjects of research as objects to be observed but as participants in the process. In 1990 Helen designed one-on-one interviews and focus groups with our former guests, and she trained volunteers to conduct them.

There had been no real research into what happens to homeless people after they leave shelters. There were plenty of anecdotes and stereotypes, usually chosen to illustrate the existing prejudices of the person recounting them. But no one really knew the answer to questions like: Once people can move on from shelters, how likely are they to get back on their feet? Do they become homeless again? Are they all on public assistance? How do their children do?

The first task was to find our former guests. We had a list of 140 who had stayed more than two weeks. Almost all those that volunteers could track down agreed to be interviewed, seventy-nine in all.

We asked three questions: What was your life like in shelter? What is your life like now? What are your hopes and dreams for the future?

More than 90 percent of the former guests described their Wellspring experience in mostly positive terms. They liked the support they got from other guests and staff, the clean, homey space, and the scenic setting with space for their children to play.

They had criticisms for us, too. For all of them, the period when they became homeless and had to come to Wellspring was the most stressful in their lives. They were in crisis. Living at Wellspring was hard. They didn't like all the rules, especially around schedules, times to get up, to eat meals, to be quiet, children's bedtimes. We knew that was tough. We also knew the schedule could be freeing as well as annoying. Once their kids were fed and asleep, they had time to work on solving their adult problems and to develop friendships with other women.

They didn't like the lack of privacy and isolated location, making it hard to go where they needed to, such as job interviews and agency appointments. Some felt becoming homeless was overwhelming enough, and too much was expected of them. There were too many meetings—housing, budgeting, individual and family therapy, twelve-step meetings, as well as general house meetings and case manager meetings.

Of all those who agreed to be interviewed, an astonishing 80 percent were still in the housing they had moved to directly from Wellspring. That showed just how stabilizing affordable housing is. More than three-quarters were receiving some kind of public assistance, but they still ran short of money after three weeks and had to eat cereal or boxed macaroni for dinner, go to the food pantry, or ask family members for help. Being on public assistance was humiliating and came at a cost in loss of control and self-esteem. One told us: "They want to crush you and grind you into the floor like a cigarette butt."

A common assumption is that homeless people "just" need to get a job, but they don't have the will to do so. That is simply untrue: 87 percent of the women interviewed said a job was their first goal. Furthermore, almost two-thirds of those with children of any age *were* working or in school, and that's out of a group in which more than 80 percent had preschoolers. The "get a job" assumption doesn't take into account the long, sad stories of struggling to earn enough money, caring for small children, all the while managing a cascade of crises. For all the women, the basic reason they became homeless was that at the time they were forced to leave one housing situation—for all sorts of reasons, such as domestic violence, abuse, family alcoholism or addictions, relationship breakups, job loss, eviction, fires, or destruction of their homes—they were unable to afford another. Most tried several temporary situations before actually becoming homeless. As one said: "Lots of things cause homelessness. Everyone has a story to tell."

One of the volunteers who conducted the interviews, Nan Araneo, recalls: "They were being asked important questions, and they really wanted to tell us. It was really empowering for them, and it changed me, too. One of my biggest takeaways was how poverty can make you prejudge someone. They so strongly wanted to create a better life for their families and themselves. I never saw anyone abusing the system. What they had to do to juggle work, school, and kids—talk about making me feel like a wimp. Many of these women were so strong and brave."

We invited the women who participated in the research to come tell their stories to the community at our symposium in May, and we paid for childcare so they could. Everyone who attended was given a copy of the research. We called it "We Are Like You," from a quote from one of the former guests in the report: "We have brains. We are like you. The only difference is that our families fell apart. If your family fell apart, then you run the risk of becoming homeless, too."

Looking out over the plenary session that day, we felt so happy to see about twenty-five of our former women guests huddled together at the front, talking excitedly to one another. We had asked Ann Louise Gilligan, our close friend who had been inspired by Wellspring and cofounded a similar center for women outside Dublin, to speak about imagination as a tool for the transformation of oppression, her dissertation topic at Boston College. Though her work was academic, and she started her talk with a history of imagination in Western philosophy going back to Plato, Aristotle, Hume, and Kant, what she said landed with the audience, especially our former guests:

"Imagination ... is feared because it doesn't belong to the stable, fixed order of things. Indeed, it threatens to destabilize this order .... Working mainly with women who live with the injustice of urban poverty, I am all too aware how injustice can stamp out the embers of hope for another kind of life, and can breed an apathy creating the belief that what is must be so .... To imagine a new world, a new way of being in the world, we must both feel intensely and image vividly."

You have to imagine what you want, see it, feel it, smell it, and make it come alive, she told us. If you can imagine it, you can do it. She asked the audience to gather into assigned groups. First, they were to feel the rage and grief of the most difficult moment of their lives, then imagine Cape Ann twenty years in the future, with all their dreams realized. They were to write, draw, and color what they wanted and needed and bring all that emotion to imagine how to make it happen.

Often at Wellspring, we heard women say, "I never thought I could dream again." They were so tired and so disappointed. Getting by day-to-day was as much as they could manage. Once we could get them into a place where they could imagine what could be possible, their dreams came spilling out. And they had the same hopes and dreams as mothers who were not homeless. They wanted careers, their own homes, enough education to get a job they liked and paid the bills, financial security, marriage, good relationships with spouses and children, and the ability to pass something on to their children.

We had a brainstorming session that led to seven working groups: First on the list was affordable housing, no surprise to us. "Housing has to be more affordable," one woman said. "I mean tons more affordable. Normal everyday jobs should be enough to buy a house." Close behind were education, jobs and businesses, childcare, domestic violence prevention (that group drew the most former guests), and spirituality. The fact folks wanted a group on this topic, which reported back that "Spirituality is the link between imagination and action," did surprise us. The last thing they shouted out was community. Those working groups met every month for the next year. After listening to all they had to say, we had our agenda for the next twenty years.

One dream screamed out clearly as our next step: education. To achieve their dreams, the women needed more education and training. What they said aligned precisely with Paulo Freire's core message: Education is the key to the transformation of poverty. We knew what we had to do next.

CHAPTER 9

Education Is the Key to the Transformation of Poverty

"I think I've got one more capital campaign in me!" Barbara Simpson, who was 80 years old and not more than five feet tall, climbed up on a chair to make this pronouncement at a board meeting. Now she had everyone's attention. "But you have to realize," she warned, "if we are asking other people for money, we have to dig deep into our own pockets!"

A decade before, Wellspring was just a group of church people, most of whom didn't even own their homes or have full-time salaries. We could barely imagine how we were going to come up with $140,000 to buy 302 Essex Street. Now we were imagining a $1 million capital campaign, in a down economy, with two other big capital campaigns going on in town.

Barbara was a powerhouse, small but mighty. We were lucky she had agreed to serve on our board. She grew up in a poor family, was orphaned at a young age, graduated as the first woman in engineering from the University of New Hampshire, and faced down local skepticism and even hostility when she started her business as the first woman cabinetmaker in Rockport. This was at a time when women couldn't get loans without a man to cosign. She built her own gorgeous one-story house with a plant conservatory. She had already worked on a successful capital campaign for the local hospital. When she retired, her pastor at the Rockport Congregational Church told her, "You've got to find something to do, and I know just the place." He sent her to Wellspring House, where she showed up asking how she could help. We gave her the job of cleaning the double-oven range. As with our staff, we asked all our board members to take a turn at all the jobs needed to make Wellspring House a home, even cleaning. Straight away she figured out the doors came off, which we had never known, making a messy job much easier. She also made furniture for us. Now she was inspiring our board to make a very big decision. They knew they were the ones who would have to make it happen.

The education working group had reported that, if we were going to help with their dreams, Wellspring needed more space for both classrooms and program offices. Wellspring was already offering some skill-building and career-planning courses. What they were imagining was much more comprehensive, courses that could move women into college and the work force, as well as prepare them as well-rounded citizens, parents, advocates, and leaders in the community. A feasibility study determined that raising $1 million—which would include $250,000 for the land trust and $100,000 for a kitchen renovation and electrical work in the house—should be doable over three years.

The board decided to name Nancy as executive director to lead the organization into this next phase of development, hired fundraising consultant Nancy Brimhall, and formed a committee to identify prospective donors. Local watercolorist Dee Parfitt, who had recently inherited some money, told us she wanted to give to Wellspring now, not in her will, and generously made a $100,000 seed donation to launch the campaign. Working with Gloucester High woodshop students, Barbara Simpson created a large sign with a sunflower stalk on our lawn called "Choosing to Grow." As donations came in, leaves were added, and bright yellow petals burst out at the top. For his donation, John Bell of Creative Professional Services in Woburn created a campaign publication called "Under One Roof," with images of Wellspring women and children by the renowned photographer Nubar Alexanian. The Kresge Foundation agreed to give us the last $250,000, once we had reached three-quarters of our goal.

We met that goal in just one year. At one point board member Anne Gifford invited a businessman she knew to meet with Nancy and development director Annie Thomas to talk about Wellspring's work. He stopped by on his way to work in Boston, expecting to make a small donation. He entered the house, passed by the baby carriages in the hall, through the kitchen where families were making breakfast, into the living room, where Nancy and Annie were waiting. A little boy still in his jammies, eating toast, with jelly all over his face, wandered in to see who was visiting. He walked right up to our prospective donor and said, "Hi!" He melted. "I can't bear it. It's like having one of my grandchildren in shelter," he told us. "How much do you have left to raise?" We told him $150,000. He said, "I'll contribute half of that."

Rosemary worked closely with architect Nick Elton to draw up a plan for a new education center that would be open and welcoming. We broke ground in May 1994, with a girls' choir singing, a dance choreographed by intern Mary Seffrood, and a talk by board president Carol Ackerman.

Life at Wellspring continued on what was now a building site, as builder Kent Ellis and plumbers Unis Brothers did their work. Outside the house, machines tossed Cape Ann's rocky boulders around like tennis balls, scooping out the hillside for the foundation. Inside, the kitchen—the hub of the house and its hospitality, where everyone passed on their way in or out—was upended for the month between Thanksgiving and Winter Solstice. Everything had to be taken out. Every spoon, every pan, every pot of jam was moved into the chapel. Some proved difficult to find later. For weeks there was no stove and no sink and no eggs for breakfast, something our guests really lamented. The fridge and toaster were moved into the tiny adjacent dining room, with a plastic curtain hung up to protect from the dust in the kitchen. Life and hospitality went on, despite the din and dust. Members of the Union Congregational Church brought a hot meal every day, as the new building took shape.

In fall 1994 the new education center was finished, with no mortgage, and we dedicated it with a big party in April 1995. We called it the Veronese Community Education Resource Center to honor Paul and Mary Jane Veronese, whose extreme generosity and faith in Wellspring had enabled our whole enterprise.

***

We wanted our education center to be a place where people in the community could gather, hold meetings, and use computers and other educational resources. But most of all we wanted to teach women. We weren't interested in just training people so they could get jobs—jobs that too often supported an inequitable system and did not pay enough to support them and their children or offer benefits like health insurance and retirement contributions. We wanted to empower them so they could help change that system: to dream, to imagine, and to find their voices and self-confidence to speak up, first in class, then in larger groups, and then at PTA meetings, board meetings, the City Council and State House, and out in the community.

In addition to Paulo Freire, two recent books had influenced us: One was *Women's Ways of Knowing*, a study that showed women's style of learning is more relational, through dialogue and connecting with others, very different from the standard classroom format of being lectured to, often with a single point of view. Another was *If Women Counted,* which calculated what the national economy would look like if all the work women did was included. Many of the women who came to us had never felt the success of completing anything. They would say: I'm just at home. I'm just a mother. Some felt they had failed at even that.

In September 1995 we began enrolling ten to twelve students at a time in a one-semester program we called Foundations. There was no tuition, but the students had to arrange their own transportation and childcare. Foundations was a big commitment, much like a college semester, seven courses spread out over five days a week, meeting from 8:45 a.m. to 2:15 p.m., for seventeen weeks. Four of the courses—English Composition, Computer Science, Women's History and Leadership, and Personal Success—could earn students twelve credits at North Shore Community College. The program also included a basic Math class, Career Development, and a Mentoring seminar. Students who didn't have a high school diploma could study for their graduation equivalency exam after 2:45 p.m.

The first thing students saw when they arrived in the classroom was a banner with the prophetic words of Susan B. Anthony: "Failure is impossible." Program coordinator Susan Hershey would start each day with a poem or a reading and ask if anyone would like to share what was going on in their lives. Many of the women were in tough family situations, widowed, single mothers, on welfare. They learned to really listen during this daily sharing time, without judgment, and to support one another. Out of that a truly caring community developed each semester. Many kept in touch with one another long after.

We organized the courses around techniques that suited women's learning styles—small group work, role playing, case studies, simulations, self-evaluations, and field trips; with less focus on lectures, reading, papers, tests, and grading.

One assignment in the Personal Success class was to take a risk. Each student chose something she found hard personally and reported back to the class. One woman took herself to a fancy restaurant alone. A student who had a fear of getting lost—this was before GPS—found her way to a teacher's house in a neighboring town for a cup of tea, with just an address and a map. Another finished and presented an artistic painting that her family had ridiculed. Yet another announced to her husband and son that she wasn't doing their dishes anymore. Her comical report back to the class was from the point of view of a fruit fly she called José. Once students broke through their fears, they asked: What else can I do? The woman who wrote about the fruit fly left her job and got one she liked more.

In the Career Development class, students drew a life map—with photos, clippings, a metaphorical car ride, however they wanted—and then shared the qualities and strengths they had gained on their journey. One student remarked, "I have never in my life given myself this much thought." A widowed mother and her adult daughter taking the class each told their life stories. Years before, their family's house burned down. The mother blamed herself, but the daughter saw her mother as a role model, holding the family together in a crisis. There were always lots of tears during this assignment.

"We learned from them, too," remembers Diane Amelia Read, who taught Career Development. "A great takeaway for me was that my life experience is not the only life experience. Someone with a differing opinion could have a wildly different experience. I don't need to judge it. I keep a stickie on my desk even now that says: When am I making assumptions when I should be asking questions?"

Nancy was thrilled to return to one of her first loves, teaching. She co-taught Women's History and Leadership with Nancy Goodman, who also was the coordinator of the education program. Students learned about the battles their foremothers had waged to get the vote, to keep their own children after a divorce, and to be paid a decent wage. They learned about St Hilda of Whitby, who led monasteries of women and men and championed education in the seventh century, and how women were considered property not that long ago in the United States.

We took students to the preserved textile mills and museum in nearby Lowell, where girls and women had worked long hours for very little. Many sent money home to their northern New England hometowns so their brothers could go to college. Originally the mill owners had wanted to produce fabric more humanely than the notoriously abusive mills in England. But after several economic downturns, they cut their female workers' pay—already less than what men would have been paid—by 25 percent and increased their hours. The company controlled their female workers' whole lives: signing them in and out, monitoring their social lives, and rationing their food. The women were responsible for running and repairing the treacherous machines. Sometimes their hair or fingers or arms got caught. With no provision for medical care, they would lose their jobs if they couldn't work. If they were late or their machine went down, their pay was docked. Pushed to the breaking point, the workers organized big strikes. Their courage contributed to the origins of the labor movement and child labor laws.

The story of business owners squeezing as much as they could out of workers struck a chord with our students. They loved the "Bread and Roses" song the mill strikers sang and learned the version by Judy Collins popular at the time. Each day leaving the classroom, they lustily sang: "Yes, it is bread we fight for, but we fight for roses, too." At graduation each student received a rose.

We took them to Commonwealth Avenue and Gloucester Street in Boston to see the statues of three women who had shaped the city's history: writer and influencer Abigail Adams, abolitionist and suffragist Lucy Stone, and African American poet Phillis Wheatley. Their final project was to choose a woman who personally inspired them. Many chose women they had studied in class—Susan B. Anthony, Elizabeth Cady Stanton, Rosa Parks, Sarah and Angelina Grimké, Anne Hutchinson, Jane Addams, Harriet Tubman, Rachel Carson, Georgia O'Keeffe, Margaret Sanger, Sally Ride. Some chose their mothers or other women in their own lives. The assignment was to write a paper and design a commemorative plate, inspired by Judy Chicago's *Dinner Party,* to be fired and glazed in the education center's kiln. Susan Hershey and Kate Seidman, both potters, taught them to pinch the clay, paint, and glaze the plates. There were always gasps of delight when their creations came out of the kiln and relief that they hadn't cracked. Then the students planned a luncheon, with tablecloths, candles, and flowers, and brought their plates. Nancy Schwoyer would ask: "You've brought twelve women with you. Do you want to talk about them?" After the luncheon we displayed the plates in the education center.

We wanted women to know their history and how hard women worked to get voting and other rights. We took them to register to vote and taught them basic civics: the platforms of the political parties and what offices would be on the ballot. A key message of the class was to become active citizens and not take those rights for granted.

"Foundations was well named," Nancy Goodman reflects now. "I came from a middle-class family that valued education, always voted, and took me to museums and plays. Working at the education center, I realized what a hugely rich foundation my upbringing gave me. Many of the students came from families where all the energy had to go into putting food on the table or holding on to their homes, so they didn't have to move all the time. We were backfilling all that culture and history."

We never knew when a particular lesson was going to connect with a student. One student who suffered from depression always had her head on her desk. One day we watched a video about Susan B. Anthony persuading three young male poll workers to register her and accept her vote in 1872, which was against the law. She was arrested, indicted, tried, and convicted, but refused to pay the fine because it would be admitting she was guilty. "And I'm not guilty!" Anthony said. At that moment the student lifted her head slowly, sat straight up and said, "If Susan B. Anthony can do it, I can do it." She started using her voice in class and others were soon looking up to her as a leader.

Some of the teachers volunteered their time and wisdom. Retired teacher Cill Triebs and Jane Saltonstall, who at age 65 had gotten her master's in education, co-taught English Composition at the center for ten years. Cill also taught Math. The two close friends often arrived wearing similar outfits, unplanned, to both their own and their students' amusement. They got the women students to write twenty minutes in their journals every day. Jane, whose father was an eye doctor, believed people often don't learn because they can't see. Every semester she arranged eye tests for the students and bought them glasses if they needed them.

At the end of the semester, volunteers from the community put the students through four one-on-one mock interviews in two hours, like speed dating. Pairs would be huddled together in every nook and cranny throughout the education center. The students came in terrified: What will I wear? What will I say? Here's my resume. Is it good enough?

The interviewers gave them immediate feedback: This is what you did well. Here's where you could use improvement. Maybe even, I would totally hire you. Occasionally students got internships right then. After two hours the students came out radiant, confident, and feeling experienced in a way they hadn't at the start of the day: I nailed it. He said he'd hire me. She said I was awesome.

***

In the education center's second year, we invited Katherine Zappone and Ann Louise Gilligan to be our Scholars in Residence. From the moment they had walked through our door back in 1981, we instantly recognized how our dreams were interwoven. They had studied education and liberation theology with many of the same professors as Nancy and Marygrace, people like Paulo Freire and Gustavo Gutiérrez at Boston College. During their years of academic study, they had become acutely aware of the gap between their own educational opportunities and those of women who had little chance of getting into a university, especially in Ann Louise's home country of Ireland. Ann Louise had seen how Irish women carried a double burden, both economic and gender oppression, even though many were the breadwinners in their households. Yet because of the patriarchal nature of living in a theocracy and how they were taught in the educational system, they were seen as secondary to men. Their children had little more chance than they did.

Like us, Katherine and Ann Louise wanted to share what they had with those who didn't have as much. Their dream was to start an educational center that would seek to break that cycle of intergenerational poverty.

While still writing their dissertations, they moved to the small house that Ann Louise had inherited from her mother in Dublin and started the search for a place that could be both their home and an education center. After two years, they found an old cedar hunting lodge called The Shanty, in a beautiful rural setting on the outskirts of Dublin. Raising funds through bake sales and other local events, they were able in 1986 to offer their first free course called Personal Development one morning a week in their sitting room. Eleven women attended from nearby Jobstown. As Dublin had become gentrified, many poor and working-class people had been displaced into newly erected government housing projects in places like Jobstown, which had almost no community infrastructure, public transportation, shops, gathering places, or other services. Ann Louise and Katherine arranged for the women students to drop off their children at a childcare center and provided a bus for the ten-minute ride to The Shanty. The short ride felt like going on adventure, escaping the confinement and isolation of their lives, the students told them. "We wanted to bring the women to a beautiful setting that would promote freedom from sexism, classism, and other inequality, so they could see a different path for themselves," Katherine remembers. Though Ann Louise and Katherine, like us, had broken ties to the Catholic Church, they wanted their center to be spiritual as well as educational, with "a table open to all—for food, drink, compassion, merriment, visioning, storytelling, and decision making," they later wrote in their book *Our Lives Out Loud*.

That first course was based on assertiveness training, a hugely popular topic with women of all class levels in the 1980s. At the Shanty, they also wanted to make sure there was time for reflection. The students could talk, without shame, about what their lives were really like and share what they needed and what they dreamed of. Those early students asked for help with household budgeting and cooking skills, so they included that in the course. Even today students still love to make Ann Louise's scone recipe that those first students learned in their kitchen.

Eventually Katherine and Ann Louise raised enough money to convert the four-car garage behind the house, which they called The Muse, into two training rooms and a kitchen for sharing meals and, of course, tea and scones. Their focus turned to economic independence for women and small businesses where women could lead. They brought in an Irish textile artist who taught hand felting and started a craft workshop called Weaving Dreams at her studio nearby. There women made toys, slippers, and other garments to sell and supplement their state benefits. Later they settled on early education and childcare centers as a great economic match where their students could work and learn to manage a business.

Demand for their classes for bookkeeping, computer skills, college preparation, literacy, community leadership, and the perennially popular Personal Development class kept growing. They found more learning spaces in community centers in the growing suburb of Tallaght but needed even more. Women of very different classes joined together to locate land and funding to build a three-story center right in the center of Jobstown. The local state authority agreed to lease a plot of land at a nominal fee and to provide architects—if the group could raise £1 million over the next year to build it. They held fund-raisers, asked nearly every large Irish corporation for donations, and lobbied politicians and cabinet members in Dublin. But at the end of the year, they had only about a third of what they needed. After the graduation ceremony that year, women, men, and children planned to march the eight miles from the Jobstown Community Center to the Dáil (Irish Parliament), hand in a letter of protest, and set up a tent city until the government provided the rest of the money. Just as graduation ceremonies were ending, the doors of the community center burst open. The Minister for Local Development strode in, leaped on the stage, and announced, "You have your money." That afternoon in a special meeting, Cabinet members had agreed to grant £600,000 to build the center. It was just as Ann Louise always said: "If you can imagine it, you can do it."

They named the new center An Cosán, the Irish word for The Path, a path that would lead women out of poverty through education. They filled it with homey furniture, not desks and chairs, because they knew from The Shanty that setting would be most comfortable for their women students. One area of the three-story building was called Rainbow House, where women attending classes could leave their children. It also provided childcare for special-needs children from the greater community. Today An Cosán offers everything from basic classes in digital skills all the way to bachelor's degree programs in community development and early childhood care and education.

In the beginning the state educational system didn't view what An Cosán was doing as real education. It was seen as something to keep women busy and give them some skills to earn extra money for their families. Ann Louise and Katherine fought to have the kind of community education they had developed be formally recognized as a comprehensive program that educated women to be full participants in society. They achieved that.

The family of Anne Genockey, now a deputy chief executive officer at An Cosán, is one proof of the success of its adult community education approach to breaking intergenerational poverty. Anne was one of their first students. She came first for computer classes, then took bookkeeping and art. She just kept taking classes, bringing her young son Darragh to Rainbow House so she could study. Eventually Anne got a master's degree in early childcare and education from the National University in Galway. She has helped start some of the eight other early childhood education and care centers owned by An Cosán around the Dublin area, which now serve more than a thousand families. Her adult children have succeeded, too. Darragh is now a manager of a large international car-sharing company, and her daughter Martina became deputy mayor of Jobstown and served on the An Cosán board.

As An Cosán flourished, Katherine and Ann Louise stepped down from leadership to pursue their careers in education, policymaking, and politics. We saw an opportunity. Our two sister organizations were closely aligned, and so was our friendship. Ann Louise and Rosemary loved to spend hours together in the garden dreaming and imagining, while Nancy and Katherine would be off plotting and planning somewhere inside. We had started with offering hospitality and shelter, and they had started with education. Now it was our turn to learn from their work. We were thrilled when they accepted our offer to be Scholars in Residence, because we knew how much we'd learn but also because of the delicious time we'd have together.

That year Ann Louise taught a course called Changing Ourselves, Changing Our World to the Foundations class in the new education center. She introduced the students, who had all left formal education early, to extremely challenging thinkers and dense texts. One was Luce Irigaray, the French feminist philosopher who critiqued *phallocentrism* in Western philosophers such as Freud, Plato, Aristotle, Descartes, and Kant. Irigaray argued that for women to be fully included as thinkers and society members, both language and culture must change. Ann Louise had a way of breaking down these theorists into common language. She would ask the women a series of questions about their own lives, for example: How were you told to be a mother? How would you like to be a mother? How does being female help you in your mothering? Then she invited them to journal or sketch their thoughts for fifteen minutes. She introduced art forms ranging from poetry to music to mythology to spark more discussions on what must change, both personally and societally. They had wonderful conversations and debates. Any of the students could have walked out of the class and discussed these intellectual thinkers and artists at a dinner party, and also applied them to their own lives. And they did.

In that class and others, we all observed the students beginning to dream about the changes they wanted to make for themselves and their children. In their evaluations, the students told us that the program helped them "replace old negative thinking with new empowered and hopeful thinking." They learned to love themselves again and learned new skills: to communicate better, to be more organized, and to overcome their fear of failure. Some decided to volunteer at Wellspring. Some said they were getting more involved in their children's school, at church, and in the community. They had plans of going to college, getting a master's, getting jobs they liked more, such as working with animals or using their artistic skills.

When we had reached out to former shelter guests for the "We Are Like You" research in 1991, women resoundingly told us: I need education. I need to learn so I can get a better job. Most said they wanted to do something to better the lives of women, such as working as a therapist for abused women or a lawyer specializing in women's rights. It was heartening to hear echoes of those same dreams with our graduates and know they had moved closer to realizing them.

But that year, 1996, their hopes turned to despair. President Bill Clinton signed a draconian "Welfare to Work" bill, authored by Representative John Kasich. It limited welfare benefits to eighteen months, after which recipients would have to get a job to continue receiving benefits. Policymakers in Washington said the bill was a "reassertion of America's work ethic" and would "break the cycle in dependency." But to those on the ground, struggling to get out of poverty, it was devastating. Any jobs our students could get wouldn't pay much. Many would have to work more than one low-paying full-time job just to provide for their children. That would leave no time to pursue a college degree, which could lead to a better job with better pay. The bill also put more pressure on community education programs like ours to prove that our courses for low-income women were directly relevant to job training. We joined other advocates at the Massachusetts State House and for a time got our students enough state benefits to complete a four-year undergraduate degree.

***

Right around this same time, an academic and social worker came into our lives who influenced us for years to come. Donna Haig Friedman was studying what living in a shelter was like for families with preschool children, for her doctoral dissertation at Brandeis University. Since the explosion of family homelessness resulting from the Reagan administration policies of the 1980s, there was very little information about how the whole shelter system had evolved and what was happening inside it. She asked if she could come observe what we did and stayed overnight several times. Donna learned from studying Wellspring, and we learned, too, from her insights into shelters, homelessness, poverty, and public policy. She also became one of our closest friends.

Before starting her doctoral program, Donna had worked in the human-service field for twenty-five years, first as a young social-justice advocate in Appalachia and then as a family advocate in programs that served families with very limited resources. She and her colleagues believed, as we did, that you learn from the families what they need. As she said, you respect that they are capable and the drivers of their own lives. That approach came straight from the early work of Jane Addams, who is often credited as the founder of social work. Addams built the first park and playground alongside her settlement houses and made sure the children had piano lessons and places to do homework—because that's what families said they needed. Addams understood that poverty and homelessness were due to forces larger than any one family. She certainly would have rejected the attitude that had taken hold a century later that "These people need to change" or "They caused themselves to be in this situation." And Jane Addams would have been appalled by the way social work was too often run by top-down professionals, telling poor people what services they needed and what hoops they needed to jump through to get them.

When Donna first saw the shared living spaces in the shelter system in the 1990s, she was shocked. When families first walk through a shelter's door, they have typically exhausted all other options. Giving up their autonomy for a while may seem a worthwhile tradeoff for beds and food for their children. But if they end up staying very long in a shelter, that gets old fast. All shelters must have rules, but in many of the shelters, she saw that families' lives were micromanaged, with very little parental choice. Parents often had to agree to hours of meetings and classes on parenting, budgeting, nutrition, and searching for housing. In some shelters, they had to rise at a certain time, be back by curfew, with prescribed bedtimes, sometimes for adults as well as children. They might be required to cook on a rotating basis, or they might be forbidden to eat with other families, share babysitting, or visit the rooms of friends they made. They might have to ask permission to hire a babysitter or get a pass to go out on the weekend. They felt their parenting was always being watched. One shelter required a staff person to unlock a medication box and watch the mother give the aspirin or antibiotic, and make sure the child swallowed it, right in the business office. Donna heard professional staff using othering language such as "women like you" and yelling at an adult shelter client, "Have you cleaned the kitchen?" in front of not just her children, but other mothers and children. One mother described being told that she needed to keep a better eye on her running toddler, later commenting to Donna that she could always spot a human service worker by the incessant use of the word "need." They began to doubt their own parenting abilities. Parents in some shelters felt they were treated as children in ways that caused their own children to lose respect for them. One of the most stigmatizing examples at one shelter was that if a parent violated a rule, they had to pick an unpleasant cleaning task written on a piece a paper from a jar, like picking the cigarette butts out of the garden, and had twenty-four hours to complete it. The late Zenobia Embry-Nimmer, a well-known anti-poverty advocate, put it this way: "In the two years I was homeless, the main thing that was reinforced within me was that I was not worthwhile, that I did not belong, not only to the community, but maybe even to humankind."

Donna called her research *Parenting in Public* and published it as a book in 2000. She interviewed fifty-five shelter directors in the state and ranked their shelters on a spectrum—from a model based on family strength to one that was professionally driven. She wrote about Wellspring as a case study of the family-strength model.

As soon as she walked in Wellspring's front door, Donna wrote, she felt the welcoming atmosphere. It felt like an old country inn—homey, warm, and comfortable. Aromas of soup and homemade bread filled the air. She noticed there were no signs saying Staff Only or listing the shelter rules, only some reminders about conserving water. She remarked that she couldn't tell who was a staff person, a volunteer, or a shelter guest when everyone gathered at the long wooden tables on the sunporch for lunch and dinner. One person offered a blessing, expressing gratitude for each person there and the hope the families would find housing. Volunteers prepared hot meals twice a day. Mothers could cook, or help in the garden, if they wanted. One mother was working up to the challenge by collecting recipes. Another mother wasn't comfortable feeding her children in a large group, so her family was allowed to eat early. In contrast to shelters that required parents to cook for large groups and determined where, when, and with whom to eat meals, Donna observed that Wellspring seemed to be respectful of a person's readiness to take on a challenge, her interest in a task, and her family's needs. In fact, she said, in no other organization that she studied did she find families treated with such respect.

Donna also wrote about the interactions she saw between Wellspring staff and stressed mothers and kids—staff members comforting a mother in tears, being a nonjudgmental listener, laughing with a mother when her child did something lovable or funny, or commenting on acts of kindness among the mothers and children. Every time a staff member was near a child, Donna witnessed her saying something complimentary about the child's special qualities and using affectionate words like "sweet pea." Smiles and hugs were freely given out, to mothers as well as children. "I felt the contagious energy that comes from being with men and women who believed in the value of their work," she wrote. "I left feeling very good about this place and the ways in which this staff interacted with families. The atmosphere was one of calmness, productive activity, and respectful relationships."

***

"If you had the funds, what would you do to end family homelessness?" Melinda Marble, director of the Paul and Phyllis Fireman Charitable Foundation, was asking that question of Nancy Schwoyer and Sister Margaret Leonard, director of Project Hope in the Roxbury neighborhood of Boston. The Fireman family was looking for a focus for their foundation's giving. Paul Fireman had grown up in the working-class city of Brockton, Massachusetts, selling sneakers and shoes out of the trunk of his car to support his family. A self-made billionaire, he had gone on to found the Reebok International shoe company.

Nancy and Sister Margaret both agreed on their answer to the question: Homeless women need to be the leaders in ending homelessness. If they are going to sit at the table with the decision makers, they must have college educations.

The Fireman family asked Nancy and Sister Margaret to meet with them. We asked if we could invite some of our shelter guests. We all trooped into their Boston office and sat around a table over Chinese takeout. The women told their stories of how they had become homeless, how they were forced to leave one housing situation and unable to find another. That became a hole that seemed impossible to dig out of. In order to afford housing, they needed a job that paid enough, and in order to get that, they needed more education. But most of the jobs they could find were so low paying that they had to work long hours or more than one to make ends meet, and that left no time for schooling.

When they were done, Phyllis Fireman, who had grown up in a blue-collar family in Brockton, looked at her husband, Paul, and grown children and said, "This could be us. It could have happened to any of us. We're all one family. I think we should fund a program to make it possible for these women to get higher education." That was the beginning of One Family

Scholars. Project Hope Boston and Wellspring House were the first two sites. Melissa Buchanan was hired as the first director.

The premise behind the One Family Scholars Program was that higher education for women who were poor would not only improve their earning ability but also change their self-perception and release talent and ability. The program was a fellowship rather than an aid program, so that recipients felt they were receiving an honor that came with responsibilities. In addition to scholarships and mentoring, the crucial component was leadership training to help end the injustice of homelessness. One Family Scholars would be women who knew from experience what was wrong, could critique it, and be a force for change. It is hard to exaggerate what it meant to the women who were selected.

Sister Margaret and Nancy knew well that this would be a hard road for women in their shelters, who were almost all mothers on welfare. The welfare program required them to have jobs or prove each week that they had been actively looking for both jobs and housing. If they were accepted to college, they might get a scholarship or aid to cover tuition. But other financial needs would increase: more childcare, textbooks, lab fees, transportation to get to work and school. Cars, trains, and buses were a big expense for them. Each Scholar reapplied each year, showing their budget for income, welfare benefits, and expenses. The site coordinator for Wellspring for ten years, Gail Mountain, helped the Scholars with budgeting but also met with them monthly to support them in all sorts of challenges: family illness, unexpected debt, loss of childcare, or just discouragement and fatigue. Red-haired, big-hearted, and funny, Gail had grown up in Gloucester, worked as a journalist for the *Gloucester Times*, and had gotten to know Wellspring when her own adult daughter became homeless. When she saw the profound impact Wellspring had on turning her daughter's life around, Gail was determined to work for us. She started as a weekend worker, cleaning and cooking, even though she disliked cooking. When the One Family program started, we knew it was the right fit for Gail, who had seen poverty and hardship. Many Scholars would say the support of the coordinator was the most important ingredient of their success.

Each year the Scholars went on a retreat focused on building leadership skills to end family homelessness. It was a time to be away from their normal lives, at retreat centers we rented on Cape Cod, the Rhode Island coast, or other beautiful New England spots. The women could relax, walk, swim, and talk with others who were studying and working hard like they were. At one of the first retreats, the women wrote their own definition of One Family Scholars: "We are women of courage, living the vision of one family, raising our voices to create a just world for all families." The days began with a ritual of songs and poetry they planned themselves and included workshops and speakers—on women's history, climate and environment, economic inequality, state housing policy. And they wrote their own state senators and representatives for legislative action on what they had learned about.

In the late 1990s our relationship with Donna Haig Friedman and her colleagues at the University of Massachusetts helped our One Family Scholars—and the whole Wellspring community—with our policy advocacy. They helped us better understand the failure of Welfare to Work and which policies we needed to advocate for instead. Donna had become director of the university's Center for Social Policy in 1998. Like us, the Center believed that people who had experienced poverty should lead advocacy efforts and hired a woman who had lived on the streets of Boston for eleven years to run its constituency advisory group.

The premise behind Welfare to Work was that people who were poor needed deadlines to find jobs and get off public support. It was based on the same demeaning paternalistic attitudes that Donna had observed in the shelter system: that authority figures know best and have to make rules to prevent people who are poor from gaming the system. That was the exact opposite of what we had learned about the lived experience of women in poverty: what they told us they needed was education to get jobs that would support their families, and they needed enough time and support to attend classes and complete educational programs. It was another example of how policymakers seldom touch, feel, or see the impact of their decisions because the people affected by policies are not consulted and are not part of the decision making.

Economists at the Center for Social Policy, led by Randy Albelda, identified a phenomenon they called the "cliff effect." In a study of ten states, they found welfare reform did not end poverty but correlated with more hardship and even greater need for family shelters. They looked at various public support programs that were cut off when people reached certain income thresholds, such as health care, housing vouchers, food stamps, childcare, and other aid to families with children. Those cutoffs were actually a disincentive to work. For each additional dollar parents earned, they could lose a dollar's worth of support, or even more, making it feel like they were falling off a cliff. Costs of housing, food, transportation, and childcare—all the resources parents needed to work—were rising faster than wages. It was simple math that put people in a Catch-22. They could not afford to accept a promotion or more hours to work because they would end up with fewer of the basic resources they needed. The cutoffs were too soon and too sudden for families to get on their feet in the working world. Many families who were cut off were only one crisis away, a family illness or a car breakdown, from losing the jobs they had or even their homes.

"People weren't sitting around being lazy," Donna told us. "They were doing everything they could, including taking more than one job. And they were paying for what they could. People don't like taking public assistance. What you have to go through to access it could take half your week. It might seem simple, that once you make a certain amount, you shouldn't need support anymore. But it required a more holistic perspective: How do we provide the right level of the basic resources that people need to work, without punishing people on the path to cover all their costs?"

One victory the women from our programs and the Center were part of was advocating for universal health care in Massachusetts, which was signed into law by Governor Mitt Romney in 2006. Paul Fireman, a close Romney supporter, helped us with getting their voices heard. The bill then became the model of the national Affordable Care Act in 2010.

One Family had been launched in 2000 with fourteen Scholars at our two sites. By 2007 the program had 125 Scholars at seven sites, who were attending colleges across the state, and it continues today. Some of the Scholars got higher degrees and jobs in law, health care, and education. The Center for Social Policy evaluated the program for us and asked Scholars about the effect of the program on their lives—and also the effect that mothers spending so many hours studying had on their children.

The mothers questioned that question, reminding researchers what their children's lives had "normally" been like: homelessness, lack of food or clothes, drug abuse in the family, illness with no health care. Once their mother had new ambitions, one reported, "They are thriving! I'm so excited because they keep on talking about college, what college they'll be going to. And their savings accounts and birthday money, it's going in the bank for college!"

One of the Scholars became an accountant with her own business, saying she had started the program mainly because she was worried that she didn't have money and wanted to be more self-sufficient. But as she went through it, her goal began to change. Her mind was opened to leaders like Mahatma Gandhi, Oprah Winfrey, Winston Churchill, and so many others. She started thinking more creatively, reflecting on her mindset and spiritual growth, and realized she wanted to be an entrepreneur. Another reported she went from making $24,000 to $80,000 a year with her new job, and another said she went from being at risk of homelessness to owning her own home in just seven years.

Scholars did not always succeed. The program was tough, and sometimes their efforts just didn't add up to success. Failure could be not only bitter but lead to self-blaming: "I need to quit my job, stay at home, and go back on food stamps and get the fuel assistance and get the [welfare] support I need," one wrote. "I cannot keep holding on and putting my family through the sacrifice just because I want to show the world that I have a master's in social work and that I am a powerful woman, which I'm not." Some who stopped out, however, tried again and succeeded.

***

Paulo Freire developed his ideas about education when he was working with illiterate house painters in his native Brazil. The standard educational methodology didn't work. He realized that learning, understanding, and change must come through dialogue, not lecturing. And true dialogue had to come from mutual respect, love, humility, curiosity, and trust.

He asked the painters: Why are people poor? He got them thinking. It wasn't their fault.

We don't have enough money.

Why don't you have enough money?
We're not paid enough.
Who's getting the money from the jobs you're doing? And why is that?
They began to realize the system was organized to keep them poor.
The next question: What can you do about it?

Freire believed that educators, social workers, researchers, and anyone who seeks to "help" in any way must first learn to listen to and get to know those they want to help through these kinds of dialogues. We at Wellspring fully embraced that. Too often educators and others believe they have the knowledge and solutions that the people need, and their job is to convey it. That was what Freire meant by his term "banking education": teachers shoveling information into passive learners, which the economic system could later withdraw in the form of obedient and unquestioning work for those in power. He rejected that kind of education. Those who are the most knowledgeable about injustice and the solutions to it are the people who are suffering under those unjust systems.

Wellspring had embodied this way of thinking and acting from its beginning, before most of our community members had even heard of Paulo Freire. Teachers at Wellspring, both volunteer and salaried, learned to draw out students' experiences and invite them to look at those experiences in new ways. We always started with the question: Why are people poor? And eventually: What can you do about it?

Freire taught us that education is the key to the transformation of poverty. Of all the things we attempted—and there were many—one of the best decisions we made was starting the comprehensive education center. It left a legacy of women, many of them formerly homeless, who transformed themselves into professionals, advocates, and community leaders.

CHAPTER 10

A Community Ecosystem

Walking down a Gloucester street one day in the late 1980s, Nan Araneo, a Wellspring volunteer, witnessed a scene she couldn't get out of her mind. A large man pulled his car over, got out, and opened the back door. A boy about 4 years old was sleeping in the back seat. The man roughly grabbed him by the arm and hauled him out on the sidewalk. He was clearly hurting the boy. The little boy was sobbing and wailing. "The guy was scary," Nan remembers.

She kept thinking about the incident. Was there anything she could have done? She looked in the Yellow Pages. She asked around. No one was working on child abuse prevention in Gloucester. She put an ad in the local newspaper and put up notices around town, asking anybody concerned about the issue to meet at the library. A half dozen people showed up, and they kept meeting. They learned about a program called Parent Aide in Denver, which sounded like what they wanted to do. Volunteers were trained and supervised, then matched for one year to meet with a parent under stress to offer support. A leader of the Denver group flew out to meet with them. They also met with Tony Tigno from the social-services department in nearby Beverly, which served Gloucester, for advice.

"If you're going to raise money to start an organization like that," Tony told them, "you have to have an umbrella agency." A lightbulb went on, Nan remembers. The next time she was at the house making lunch for guests and staff, she asked Nancy if Wellspring could be that umbrella.

The board talked it over for some time, going back to the mission statement. Wellspring was about providing shelter, housing, economic opportunity, and education. We placed our faith in one another's capacity and lifted up people's strengths, not their deficiencies. One concern was that anyone who asked for a Parent Aide would be labeled neglectful or abusive. That didn't fit Wellspring. As it turned out, another Wellspring volunteer, Anne Gifford, had previously volunteered with a Parent Aide group run by Catholic Charities in another town, and she helped allay that concern. In the end, we decided that a community-based, volunteer model to support parents under stress, so that everybody would be safe in the family, was indeed a good fit with Wellspring's mission.

Charitable organizations are expected to find their "niche" in the nonprofit world and stick to it, and Wellspring didn't do niches. Radical hospitality was about not accepting limits, stretching our hospitality, and always widening our circle. Parent Aide was an example of that.

A working group was formed and helped hire a part-time director, Rebecca Koch, to recruit, train, and supervise volunteers and match them with parents requesting support. In 1991 Parent Aide was funded as a program in Wellspring's budget and was given office space in the new education center. A six-week training helped aides learn to set boundaries. "You were there as a friend, period—not a chauffeur, bank, or babysitter," Nan remembers. If a parent said to an aide, "I need money," we encouraged them to ask, "What can I do to help? I can't give you money. I can imagine you're running out of money when this is all you get in food stamps. Would you like a ride to the food pantry?" That created a space for a conversation that could go deeper, say, about the judgment that food stamp recipients feel in the cashier line, and a chance to affirm they have a right to buy what they need and want. Those kinds of conversations would not happen if an aide simply put a hand in her pocket and offered money.

Two mothers whom Nan was paired with at different times had to move out of their homes, one because of fire, another because of lead paint. Nan used her connections to help find them other places to live. She enlisted her husband, kids, and her family's truck to help them move. Other times she accompanied mothers to court to get a restraining order from ex-husbands or boyfriends, or helped them find drug treatment or therapy. For many people, it was the first time they had ever had someone to support them in those ways. The bond between parents and aides often became very strong. Even today when Nan runs into one of her parents from decades ago, they greet her with a big hug and tell her all about their now-grown kids.

One formerly homeless mother of four young children was so scared, nervous, and shy that her aide had to visit several times before she'd let her come inside the apartment. That wasn't unusual. Even though the parents requested an aide, they often had deeply mixed feelings about letting someone they didn't know into their homes and their private lives and around their children.

Within just a few years, this little program that started with a kernel of inspiration from one of our volunteers grew into a comprehensive parent-support program that touched lives throughout the Cape Ann community: hundreds of parents, children, and a vast number of volunteers. It was exactly the kind of thing we had dreamed of when we had come up with our mission statement to "participate in social change ... rooted in community needs."

Parent Aide continually held new trainings for its volunteers, who also met weekly with the director and other aides to talk about whatever was happening and how to handle it. They all were constantly reflecting on all they were seeing and learning about the needs of parents and children in our community and brainstorming how to better meet them.

In 1995 Rebecca Koch started a second program called Family Nurturing for families with children ages 5–12. Through discussions, videos, exercises, children's art activities, and a shared pizza dinner once a week, the fifteen-week program helped families set new parental expectations, learn alternatives to physical punishment, and practice how all members of a family could nurture one another. We spent the first week corralling kids running through the stairways till we got our classroom management system down. But we absolutely loved how much life and energy they brought to the education center.

As the program grew, it renamed itself Cape Ann Families and moved into a big property at 28 Emerson Avenue, owned by a local businessman, Ed Anderson. He first rented to us, then sold the building to Wellspring for half the commercial price. The building with its big central hall had plenty of room for kids and families to move around. It also became the home of Wellspring's economic development office, holiday store, food pantry, and The Open Door, which offered a hot meal there every day, after we renovated it with a well-equipped kitchen.

In 1996 Stacy Randell began as director of Cape Ann Families and started an ongoing, year-round support group called the Parent Connection, to help keep those healthy relationships that had been developed in the Family Nurturing course going. Some parents had come from abusive or neglectful homes, and most had been raised with physical punishment. Many believed that's what good parents did.

One woman, who had adopted her grandson after her daughter's addiction made her unable to care for him, came into the program with the attitude, "I know how to do this. This is what you have to do keep kids in line." Facilitators observed how she spoke to her grandson in a harsh, belittling way, heavy with sarcasm. They talked about how *sarcasm* comes from a Greek word *sarkazein*, which means "tearing flesh from the bone," and how damaging it could be. Over time parents came to conclusions themselves about nurturing and told us in their evaluations: "I am not an army sergeant. I should not give orders and expect compliance." "Children are more loving when there are boundaries." "Taking care of ME is as important as taking care of THEM." "About the spanking thing: I never realized how it hurts a kid's self-esteem."

From there, the number of new initiatives just exploded. As ideas bubbled up, Stacy and her volunteer team put them into action, one by one.

- A Teen Mentoring program trained and matched teens with younger children.
- A Teen Summit group planned youth band fund-raisers, dances, teen/cop dialogues, a cleanup of a local pond, with "We're Fond of Our Pond" bumper stickers.
- A partnership with the Institute for Child and Adolescent Development served children whose development was impacted by trauma.
- A support group formed just for fathers.
- School vacation programs were filled with arts, puppet shows, games, crafts, songs, and healthy snacks.
- A self-portrait workshop for schoolchildren with artist Robert Shetterly, based on his "Americans Who Tell the Truth" series, produced notecards with the children's art as a fund-raiser.
- Annual awards for the Parent, the Child, and the Family Supporter of the Year, with the theme "Who I Am Makes a Difference," highlighted the importance of praise in healthy families. That one borrowed an idea from the *Chicken Soup for the Soul* series, a blue-ribbon

ceremony that charged each person who was honored to acknowledge two other people in their lives who were deserving of praise.

Parent Aide was like a spark that caught fire to light up the whole community.

***

From Wellspring's start, we wanted to be deeply woven into the larger community. We wanted to be interdependent, paying our share of city services we received, buying what we needed locally as much as we could, and providing needed services ourselves—in short, contributing to a healthy local community ecosystem.

During our first forum in 1991, we had listened to the hopes and dreams of formerly homeless women in the research "We Are Like You." That gave us the charge to raise $1 million to build the Veronese Community Education Resource Center and help those women realize their dreams. Five years later, we were ready to focus not on Wellspring as an organization and its growth, but on Wellspring's role in the place we called home, Cape Ann. Once again, we turned to the Freirean Action/Reflection model, reflecting on the past in order to empower the future.

We publicized all over Cape Ann that we were hosting a two-day forum on "Choosing the Future" in January 1996. We were bowled over when 140 people from all parts of the greater Cape Ann community registered, again many of whom would have had little opportunity to cross paths otherwise—people of different ages, from different cities and towns, with different backgrounds, interests, and personalities; bankers, fishing families, businesspeople, health professionals, artists, ministers, government workers, teachers, students, as well as our own board members, staff, volunteers, and program participants.

We asked our dear friends Ann Louise and Katherine, who were still with us as our Scholars in Residence, to facilitate. They set the stage by revisiting Ann Louise's work on memory. "I believe that each one of us has within him or her a memory which not only can provide answers to our own present search for meaning but which can also offer insight as to the shape of a viable community …" Ann Louise told those assembled. "I believe that there is a deep connection between memory and imagination. As we share recollected moments, rich memories, we will begin to imagine the unimaginable." A powerful and charming speaker, Ann Louise combined intellect, radical feminism, her Irish accent, and her gentle, loving spirit in a way that engaged the whole room, from the poorest single mothers to the most powerful men in the city. She fearlessly declared that the world has been too much shaped by men's approach of setting goals, as if that's the universal way of looking forward. She urged women "to bring to birth, nourish, and above all give voice to their way of imagining the world." It was a message that especially excited Wellspring staff, volunteers, guests, and program participants.

People shared their own memories, but also those of their grandparents and older relatives, bringing their wisdom and continuity into the conversations. They talked about families and neighborhoods on Cape Ann, working hard, sharing what they had, enjoying good times, and helping one another through bad ones. There also shared sad and angry memories: of native culture being lost, of prejudice, discrimination, racism, sexism, and distrust of outsiders.

When the participants broke into small groups to identify the most important value needed to work toward a viable community, those groups reported back one common theme, over and over: welcoming of differences.

Finally, we asked the 140 people from throughout our community to imagine the Cape Ann they'd like to see sustained into the future. Almost every group mentioned concern for the fishing community. They also brainstormed creative ideas to revitalize our local economy and businesses, keep work and money in the community, bring more diversity to education and arts opportunities, protect our fragile coastal environment, preserve Gloucester's beautiful harbor in a way that balanced fishing and tourism, expand public transportation and affordable housing, among many others.

Once again, as at our first forum, we formed working groups, thirteen in all, to act on the ideas and pledges we had made.

As in 1991, we paired the forum with a Participative Action Research (PAR) project, this time run by Katherine. Students in the Foundations course, who had lived through the same struggles as the income-limited women they interviewed throughout Cape Ann, helped design and conduct the research. In one-on-one interviews, they heard about women who would like to get their GED (graduate equivalency degree, or high school diploma) or a business degree to get a better job, but couldn't go to night courses with no buses or childcare available. One woman told how her child's stroller was her only transportation to get to the laundromat and how she hoped it held up under the heavy bags of laundry. The researchers brainstormed solutions that wouldn't be costly and where volunteers could help: shared cooperative carpooling, a phone center where women seeking jobs could receive calls, a resource guide that had all the information about where to get help in one place. They spelled out the need to take on larger policy solutions through advocacy, such as rethinking welfare and improving public transportation. "The greater our ability as a community to strengthen our neighbors' economic standing, the stronger, healthier, and more independent our whole community will become," they concluded in the final report called "We Love This Place."

Wellspring didn't have the capacity to do it all. This time, we hired Nancy Goodman to direct what we called Cape Ann Sustainable Communities. For the next two years, she helped keep the pledges and goals organized, coordinated those initiatives, and opened up our education center as a place to meet, whether the work ended up as Wellspring-sponsored or independent community projects.

***

"How many of you still go down and try to buy scrod?" Angela Sanfilippo implored the group at our 1996 forum. Scrod was the New England term for a small cod or haddock. "When you buy scrod," she explained, "it's a piece of fish that is smaller than the legal size that US fishermen are allowed to bring in. It's imported from Canada and other places. But our men cannot bring it in. They have to throw it overboard…. Every Gloucester fisherman, when he comes home, he says: 'This is a sin in front of God that we have to throw fish overboard.'"

Back in 1969 Angela Sanfilippo along with Lena Novello had organized the Gloucester Fishermen's Wives Association to fight for the fishing community. As multinational trawlers moved in and overfished the most popular species, the women had argued at meetings and knocked on doors to fight for the rights of local fishing families, while their husbands were at sea. These women were so respected in the community. They got improved safety standards on vessels, created a health plan for fishermen that became a model for universal health care in the state, established a marine sanctuary at Stellwagen Bank, helped out-of-work fishermen retrain, and fought to prevent oil drilling on Georges Bank and to stop natural gas terminals onshore.

Angela, the wife, daughter, and sister of fishermen, wanted to bust the myth that local fishing boats were depleting the ocean and abusing the fish. She wanted the people of Gloucester to understand that buying scrod was undercutting their own community. She wanted people to learn to eat more underutilized fish, like dogfish. Dogfish are small sharks, at that time plentiful in the rich fishing grounds off Gloucester. In England the firm, flaky white meat is often used in fish and chips. People in Massachusetts used to eat it, too, along with all kinds of species the local fishermen brought in. But when food processors realized how much more they could make selling fillets of haddock, cod, and flounder, that's all they wanted to buy from the fishermen and all they sold, and for years that's what the people of Cape Ann grew accustomed to eating. Now those species are depleted.

Federal regulations restricted the species that could be landed and required that all the rest be thrown overboard—already dead. The restrictions, taken without any consultation with the fishermen who had deep knowledge of the ocean and its fish, were driving local fishing families out of business.

The Gloucester Fishermen's Wives needed help marketing the underutilized fish species like dogfish, redfish, and whiting. Wellspring joined them to start Fish to People, a nonprofit initiative that would deliver lesser-known fish to shelters, soup kitchens, and food pantries, already cleaned. It was our first community economic development project. The fishermen's wives knew that to market unfamiliar species, they had to teach people how to prepare it so it tasted good. Lena was a great cook, and Angela taught us all about the various fish. They were both delightful to spend time with. They visited soup kitchens and shelters like Wellspring, sometimes weekly, slapped a freshly caught fish on the table, and taught us how to clean it, fry it, cook it into chowder, and make fish balls. We learned that dogfish had to be cleaned almost immediately after it was caught, or it took on an intolerable urine-like smell that you couldn't cook out of it.

The project continued for about ten years, and efforts to market underutilized fish in Gloucester continue still today. It was hard for our small project to guarantee a steady supply of fish to the clients, and hauling fish was very labor intensive, not to mention messy. Our accountant Rick Flynn helped as a volunteer fish deliverer and always teased us, "I'm never going to forgive you. I can't get the smell of fish out of my car to this day!"

We felt good about our contributions. We listened to what people in our community said they needed. We agreed to try things. Not everything we tried worked out in the long term. But we kept the conversations going, and we knew the projects that came out of them contributed to the community, whether they went on for a few years or many.

One of the pledges at the 1996 forum was to develop an alternative currency exchange. Jeanne Gallo, the first director of our education center, had invited Gurunan Khalsa and Tim Mitchell of the Valley Trade Connection, in Franklin County, Massachusetts, to speak at the forum. They explained how they had created their own local currency in the Pioneer Valley in western Massachusetts. It started with the University Women's Network asking: What is something I have that I could offer other people? What is something I need that would be nice for someone to offer me?

A working group from the forum was inspired to try it on Cape Ann. Working with local banks, they printed Cape Ann Dollars that could be used only on Cape Ann for real services and goods, say, a haircut, a music lesson, a café meal, or a bike repair. The money could not be stashed in a bank or in investments, where it would create wealth only for its owner. It had to keep on being used so it would keep creating real value for things the community needed—goods, services, and income—every time it was exchanged. That has a very different impact from spending US dollars at a chain like Wal-Mart or McDonald's, where 80 percent leaves the community never to be seen again. And today, whenever you shop online, all that money leaves your community as well. The project continued for several years and got local people to think more about the impact of where they spent their dollars. Later Nancy Goodman became a leader of the Cape

Ann TimeBank, which still enables its members to trade services such as a meal, gardening, or a ride to the airport, with the currency of time.

Around the same time Wellspring learned about another program, Working Capital, that fit with the economic development ideas that our own working group was exploring. Originating with a bank that offered micro loans in India, the idea was to form peer support groups in economically disadvantaged communities, made up of people who had small businesses or were looking to start them. Gloucester qualified because of the decline in the fishing industry. One goal of the project was to help fishermen transition to land-based work. Yet we knew the economic decline due to the fishing crisis radiated throughout the community. When the fishing boats weren't going out, for example, the local laundromat that had been doing their weekly wash when they came back into port suffered, too.

At its height about eighty-five local small-business people participated in Working Capital, meeting monthly in groups of eight or so. A spa owner, a printmaker, a home-based accountant, and an aspiring restaurateur, for example, might share what they were learning about getting started and how they solved problems that came up. The program also brought in local experts in law, insurance, taxes, and accounting to give them technical support on, say, how to file their year-end reports or become a limited liability corporation. Participants could apply for micro loans up to $5,000 from a fund the program established through local banks and fundraising. Their own peer group members vetted their applications and decided whether they were a good candidate for a loan. The return rate on those loans was more than 96 percent.

Seeing the transformation of lives and its impact on our community was exciting. One lumper and deckhand who worked on the fishing boats was able to start a taxidermy business, serving sport fishermen who wanted trophies for their walls. An entrepreneur who started a home health business and another who opened a consignment shop on Main Street hired local people, and both are still going strong today.

But with the economic downturn in the early 2000s, our excited feelings about all these new programs turned more sober. Wellspring had to tighten its belt. We had taken on a lot and increased our staff from fifteen to thirty since 1996. We had to cut something. We went to the program directors, laid out the financials, and asked for their advice. We asked each to write a paper about why their program was essential to Wellspring's mission and where they could cut costs. The shelter, the education program, affordable housing, and Cape Ann Families—the board was clear that all these had to stay. It was a very tough decision. When we announced that we were closing down Working Capital, the small-business people begged us, "Please don't do this." We explained we really didn't have any other choice. We promised we would support them and patronize their businesses, and we helped out-of-work fishermen retrain. We also referred them to the Chamber of Commerce, which was starting its own initiative for new and very small businesses.

***

As we look back on all the community projects Wellspring undertook, three made the most lasting impact on Cape Ann as a viable, sustainable community for all who lived there: Cape Ann Families, then two other opportunities that came to us in the mid-2000s, the MediClerk program and the Wellspring Adult Learning Center.

Sue Beaton, who worked on advocacy for One Family, argued with us that not every woman wanted or needed a college degree, though they all did want interesting, good-paying jobs. We certainly agreed with preparing people for jobs, as long as wages were fair. One field that was crying for capable employees was medicine, which needed nonclinical administrative workers. When we approached hospitals about offering specialized training to our students, they welcomed the idea.

As an offshoot of the One Family Scholars program, the first Mediclerk Training was held at Partners North Shore Medical Center in Salem in 2001. Students learned about medical record keeping, terminology, and procedures and spent two weeks shadowing a qualified staff person. Starting salaries at that time were $15 an hour (they are higher now), with full benefits, including vacation and sick days. Nowhere else could women without bachelor's degrees get secure jobs for that kind of compensation package. One of our students wrote to us, "I can't stress enough how awesome the program had been for me. It got me started on a career where I support myself, and I feel like there is no limitation on how far I can go." Some of our students went on to become full-time health workers or doctors. The nationally accredited program, now called Healthcare Office Support Training (HOST), can be completed in fifteen weeks full-time or thirty-two weeks part-time. It continues to be offered twice a year in a partnership between Wellspring House and Salem Hospital, which is now part of the Mass General Brigham system.

***

Cape Ann has long been home to strong communities that grew out of waves of Italian, Portuguese, and Finnish immigrants in the twentieth century. Those communities welcomed and helped new immigrants from their own countries. For the most part, the larger community understood and accepted who they were and appreciated their contributions to the city's economic and cultural life.

In the mid-2000s immigration justice was reaching a crisis point in the country. Many immigrants were now coming to Gloucester, rather than just to immigration gateway cities like Boston and Worcester. People from so many countries—Kazakhstan, Guatemala, China, Congo, Ecuador, Chile, Albania, Micronesia, Egypt, Myanmar, Dominican Republic—were fleeing wars, intolerable economic crises, government repression, violence, and natural and climate disasters. Some applied for asylum or refugee status. Some had student, tourist, or other temporary visas when they arrived, then stayed when they found work or love here. And some came into the country with no documentation, at great risk to themselves and their families.

Marian Linden, who had previously served as Wellspring associate director, was concerned about the broken immigration system and the extreme hardships undocumented immigrants faced trying to help their families. Her own grandparents had immigrated from Italy around 1900, and her grandmother had never learned to speak English. She attended a weekend conference to learn more and decided she could help by teaching English as a second language (ESL). She asked to volunteer at the Adult Learning Center program at the local library, started more than a decade before by a volunteer, Maggie McBride, to help fishermen get their GEDs and jobs. The program had recently started teaching ESL as well. Maggie told Marian she wasn't taking on new students or tutors because she was retiring. She was packing her books and closing the program.

Marian suggested that Wellspring take it over. We were thrilled. Welcoming immigrants was yet another step in radical hospitality. We had long wanted a Wellspring presence in the heart of Gloucester. We knew there was so much need, so many immigrants struggling with trauma, working several jobs, sorting out all the paperwork required of them, often living with two or three families in one apartment. One of the passages of the Hebrew Bible that had always inspired us was "Love the stranger for you were once strangers in Egypt." And Jesus asked his disciples to welcome strangers just as they would welcome him: "I was a stranger and you welcomed me .... as you did it to one of the least of these my brothers, you did it to me."

We asked Melissa Buchanan, who was teaching GED at our Emerson Avenue location and fluent in Spanish, to direct the Wellspring Adult Learning Center and expanded her hours. She still directs the center, based downtown at the Sawyer Free Library, where it is a hub of the immigrant community in Gloucester (though it has been housed temporarily at an Endicott College building while the library is renovating). The students attend small classes, and the center regularly hosts get-togethers where students bring a dish from their home countries, speak in English, laugh together, and see that they're not alone.

Some students were professionals in their own countries and now face the choice of pursuing a different career path or more education in English so they can work in their field in this country. Others have minimal literacy in their first languages. Their schooling may have been interrupted by war, frequent moves, or lack of funds for tuition, transportation, and uniforms. Tutors must really get to know their students and what they're up against. Many have two or three jobs and can't do much homework outside class. Yet they won't learn English from once or twice weekly sessions with a tutor. So the tutor needs to adapt, perhaps assigning just ten vocabulary words or a few written questions.

Marian still remembers her first student, a determined young man from Central America who came to Gloucester, where he had one relative. He was working several part-time jobs at convenience stores. In addition to instructing him in grammar and vocabulary inside the library, she took him out into the city, to the post office, to stores, to coffee shops, to practice everyday interactions in English. He learned to ask for and give directions, say what he wanted to buy, or describe what he was seeing. After learning some conversational English, he a got a job with a painter. When that person retired, he started his own painting business, which is now in high demand. When Marian saw him recently, he told her he had gotten his GED and was excited to show her business books he was studying in Spanish, something he could not have done when he came to the program.

Tutors help students prepare for their written citizenship tests: twelve questions chosen randomly from a list of 100. They may also coach them about cultural nuances, for example, that it's not customary to kiss the teacher's hand, nor to address people as "Sir" or "Ma'am" except in a very few instances, or that you need to go to City Hall to get a beach sticker. Tutors might explain it's better not to say "I need a job"—even though, it's true, they do—and instead ask, "Do you have a job available? I can do this work." One student applied for a job and was told, "You ain't working here." Confused, he related the interaction to his tutor, "I know I don't work there. What did he mean?" She had the painful task of explaining that wasn't a nice way to speak, and the business owner didn't like who he was. On the whole, though, both tutors and students say, Gloucester has been a warm and hospitable place.

In 2019 Wellspring and the library mounted a photography exhibit called "Portraits of Cape Ann Immigrants," telling the stories of twenty students and teachers at the Wellspring Adult Learning Center. One student, Yasser, had been robbed and kidnapped with a knife put to his neck in Egypt, but the police did nothing. Starting at age 16, he tried for twelve years till he finally got a visa to come to the United States, but he knew only a dozen words of English. He found a job working for an Arabic-speaking convenience store owner in Gloucester. He thought it would be hard to talk to American people, but it comes easy, he says. His tutor, June, whose own grandparents immigrated from Russia (she still has the silver candlesticks they brought), says tutoring has been wonderful for her, too. "Yasser is such a hard worker. If anyone can make it, he'll make it." His wife sends in delicious meals to show the family's gratitude. A few years ago Yasser bought his own convenience store. "This is my neighborhood," he says now. "This is my country."

Diana and her family fled Guatemala after her 17-year-old daughter got in the way of a gang fight and was killed on the street "for nothing," she says. Diana cooks in a restaurant on Cape Ann. The Wellspring tutors help her with English but also with her children's schools, doctors' appointments, and directions. "When I learn, I get more confidence," she says. "Here we go to the fiesta, go out at night, nothing happens. I'm very happy now. I have my work; my kids are in school; my husband is working. It's safe here."

One of the tutors, Gonzalo, came to the United States as a graduate student from Chile decades before, also with poor English at first. He decided he wanted to stay and raise his family here. When he retired, he started tutoring students who aspired to higher education and helps with math and technology as well as English. "Working with the immigrants here," he says, "I see they are so important. Most of the work they do is totally invisible; it happens in the back rooms, in the back office. If one day they were to disappear, you would notice a large change in the level of service you get—office cleaning, nursing care. You would have to think: why is this happening? I feel grateful for this country. I came here penniless. I was poor as a rat here for a number of years, but I knew that if I kept trying, I would make it. That's what I want my students to understand."

***

Community education is a commitment to listen to the community and provide education for what the community needs. Foundations was one part, Cape Ann Families another, the Wellspring Adult Learning Center another.

Once we made the commitment in our mission statement to "participate in social change through the provision of shelter, affordable housing, local economic opportunity and education rooted in community needs," we had no choice but to be open to the ideas that came and whatever our community needed. Enlarging and building our community was an essential part of radical hospitality. We could not do everything ourselves, but what we could and did do was foster mutuality throughout the community—teachers, learners, service providers, workers, volunteers, artists, all in exchange with one another. We see that legacy still today in the programs and many personal relationships that continue.

We believe the truth is in the community. The community has its own answers, and it also has the strength and skills to make whatever it needs happen. We certainly brought in scholars and consultants to help facilitate and apply their tools, but they were all rooted in this same philosophy. We didn't believe in getting lots of degrees to do what you were called to do. We rejected the attitude based on "I'm the expert" and "You're being educated or counseled or treated or served." That was not Wellspring. The act of having regular forums, bringing 140 people together and asking what they needed, what's possible, then asking them to imagine and work together on what to do next, that was the very soul of what Wellspring was about.

CHAPTER 11

The Lights Go Out

"What is going to happen to Wellspring when you two retire? Are you planning for it?" It was the first time we'd been asked that.

Tim Dalmau was a new friend who was visiting us at Wellspring. When Rosemary had been on a lecture tour in Australia in the late 1990s, Tim had been in the audience. The founder of Dalmau Consulting was so taken by what she said about Wellspring House that he invited her to chat more over lunch under an awning on beautiful Bondi Beach. Now he was sitting in our living room at Wellspring showing us photos of his family, along with diagrams of his work with organizations as "living systems."

We really had not made any plans for a leadership transition for Wellspring. Tim said he'd like to introduce us to his colleagues, Richard and Claire Knowles. They too worked with companies, municipalities, and nonprofits to help them behave as "living systems," sharing leadership and co-creating their future, rather than functioning as a top-down, command-and-control hierarchical system.

At the time, we didn't completely understand why they all found Wellspring so fascinating. The way we worked—turning to one another as equals to sort out problems, including our shelter guests in our research and forums, and acting, reflecting, and growing in response to whatever was happening—seemed normal. We had always done what they were working to get other workplaces to try. We were a real-life model for them.

Over almost two years Dick and Claire Knowles generously donated their work with everyone in our organization. They worked with our program participants, volunteers, staff, administration, and board and helped us all gain a better understanding of Wellspring as a living system that was interdependent and adaptable.

In both teaching and learning, images often convey ideas better than words. At the end of their work with us, the Knowleses facilitated another forum for more than 100 people from the larger Wellspring community. Rosemary and shelter director Mary Martel created a visual image by pushing, pulling, and laughing a sheet of chicken wire into a four-foot-diameter bowl shape. At the forum's closing ritual, two people at a time held the wire bowl, and each person threaded a yard of satin ribbon through it, in as many colors as we could find.

This container was like our community: everyone was welcomed in, and everyone was responsible for holding up that mission of hospitality. We were all woven into a fabric that was diverse and yet clearly a whole. Dick explained that, like the ribbons in the bowl, the sum of what everyone contributed to Wellspring provided stability and focus, and at the same time provided freedom for people to do what was needed and what made sense. Like Wellspring, the bowl wasn't rigid but could change when needed. And it was permeable so new ideas and energy could be woven into it. In the coming years we kept the bowl in the Wellspring chapel, and several times a year we invited new board members and staff to weave in their own ribbons.

The work Dick and Claire did with Wellspring was all aimed at addressing the question that Tim had raised years earlier: What will happen to Wellspring when the founders leave? The Knowleses emphasized to us that if we wanted our values of mutuality and community to live on after the founders stepped down, we had to leave behind structures that would make our core principles visible and sustainable for future leaders. If we couldn't do that, Dick and Claire's report said, "there is real potential for Wellspring House to lose its uniqueness, excitement, and meaning. It would drift toward becoming a more typical social-service agency where there would be fewer volunteers, more professional staff, more bureaucracy and less effectiveness."

A 2001 editorial in the *Gloucester Daily Times* raised the question again, much more pointedly: "Will it be possible for the next generation of Wellspring leaders to keep alive the flame of feminist theology that burns in the hearts of the founders, or will this brave effort to create a new society devolve into liberal do-goodism?"

Those warnings proved prescient.

***

We were all well aware of the forces that would try to get Wellspring to conform to a more typical nonprofit structure. In 2003 the board set up a committee to study the steps needed for a smooth transition. At the heart of their reflection was the question: *What is the essence of Wellspring that must be passed on?*

We all had a clear idea of the answer: Our mission statement that each life touches every other life and that we have faith in one another's capacity. Our practice of mutuality, that we are all in community with one another, we are all helpers and helped, all teachers and learners. A commitment to "Power With," not "Power Over." And we wanted the organization to continue the priority initiatives our guests told us they needed—the shelter, affordable housing development, the education center, and support for parents, the priorities we had laid out during the recent recession.

In 2006 Rosemary resigned as associate director and clerk of the organization, roles she had held for twenty-five years. During the transition she would continue to care for the gardens and edit the newsletter.

Nancy submitted her letter of resignation as executive director effective October 31, 2007. She still felt Wellspring was her life and much more than a job. She wanted to transition to a new role to support Wellspring's mission. These were not just Nancy's plans. The board and the Transition Committee, which later became the Search Committee, were clear that they did not want the kind of transition where the outgoing director clears her desk and disappears.

A decade later an article in the *Stanford Social Innovation Review* affirmed that view: "Every year, thousands of nonprofit boards face the daunting task of hiring a successor to replace the seemingly irreplaceable: the long-serving, beloved founder. ... 'Make a clean break' goes the warning. 'Founders and successors are managerial oil and water. They just don't mix.' ... Yet, is a clean break really the best way to ensure a successful founder succession?" An in-depth quantitative study cited in the article "found that the answer is often no. To a surprising extent, transitions that extend the role of a nonprofit founder yield the best results."

The committee took several steps to transition the founders into new support roles. Those tasks included defining Nancy's role as director of legacy projects. She would fund-raise, build the endowment, and serve as a public-policy advocate and instructor of Wellspring's organizational model. Nancy, Rosemary, and Mary Jane would be directors emeritae, who would participate but not vote in board meetings. They created two legal documents. One was a notarized clerk's certificate, a resolution from the board listing their expectations of how Wellspring House Inc. would continue to manage and operate 302 Essex Avenue as a place of hospitality for homeless and limited-income people. The chapel would be a space for spiritual renewal. The grounds would be used for growing organic vegetables and flowers. The second document was a founders' lease, allowing the two of us to continue to live in the house, occupying the two upstairs bedrooms and bathroom that had been our home for decades. Marygrace, Paul, Mary Jane, and Sissy could also stay at Wellspring if they wished, and they all did at times.

Next began the search for a new director. The board hired an experienced consultant who agreed to include the founders in the search process and in future roles. Yet as the work continued, the board and all of us realized, too late, how entrenched she was in the hierarchical top-down model of leadership and the idea of a clean break between founders and successors.

The consultant started with an assessment, prepared by Non-Profit Transitions LLC, which echoed what Dick and Claires Knowles had seen: "The outside observer is immediately made aware that clients, staff, volunteers and the greater community all regard Wellspring House as a special place. Staff at all levels, board members and even volunteers unfailingly begin a discussion about Wellspring House with ringing endorsement of the mission, history, leadership and program effectiveness of Wellspring House. They are proud of its impact as a social change agent. These comments are so uniform in character and so strongly articulated as to leave little doubt of its veracity."

The board found a candidate they liked and offered her the job. However, she then revealed that she was still under contract to her current employer for another year and proposed to lead Wellspring part-time. The board said no. The search began again in the new year, 2008.

A former staff person, who had held several roles at Wellspring, had run a small business, and recently completed a master's in business administration, applied. The Search Committee was relieved. We knew she was familiar with our mission and the practice of mutuality, plus we thought she would bring financial skills that the founders had had to learn on the job. Tired and anxious to get the hiring done, the board offered her the executive director position to begin on April 1, 2008. In their negotiations, she agreed to make no major changes for a year and after that to consult with staff before any major changes. The board also hired Nancy to start in her new legacy projects position, in a new office three miles away in the Emerson Avenue building, and unanimously approved the clerk's certificate and founders' lease.

***

Nine months into the job, in January 2009, the new director ended the seventeen-week Foundations program. Since 1995, 235 women had completed the program. In its place a new eight-week program emphasized earning a high school graduate equivalency degree (GED), meeting college entrance course requirements, and job training.

Women's History, Personal Success, Career Development, and the Mentoring seminar were all dropped, as was the partnership with North Shore Community College. There were no more morning sharing times to build a community of learners. There were no more risk-taking assignments, life maps, mock interviews, journal writing, field trips, nor opportunities to create art and write while learning about great artists and writers. Paulo Freire's idea that education is the key to the transformation of poverty was no longer explicit in Wellspring's educational philosophy. Some donors reacted by withdrawing their contributions.

Also in January the director informed the board, without consulting staff, that 302 Essex Avenue would no longer house homeless families. All but one of the shelter staff positions would be eliminated. This change would save the organization $130,000 per year. The remaining three families currently living there would move to the Washington Street apartment building on February 1. Homeless families would now be housed in separate apartments, and the emphasis would be on making them independent as quickly as possible, rather than interdependent as part of a larger community. Families would no longer sit at the table for meals with other families, staff, volunteers, and board members. They would no longer have a say in any of the decisions about their time in the shelter.

The new executive director clearly had a very different idea of Wellspring from the communitarian model it had followed for twenty-five years. The absence of families at 302 Essex Ave was the strongest rejection of the model by which Wellspring had been known, putting homeless families at its center. When a board member raised a concern about the absence of community, the director replied, "Nobody wants to live in community anymore."

The once-bustling house at 302 Essex Avenue was now often dark at night. People in Gloucester noticed and remarked on it to us. In our part-time roles, we were increasing the length of our semiannual visits to England to see Rosemary's adult children and grandchildren. Back in 1989 we had taken out a mortgage to purchase a small stone cottage in Yorkshire to stay in when we visited twice a year. Rosemary didn't want to impose on her children for long visits. The family rented the cottage out to vacationers when we weren't there. Sometimes people who didn't know us that well imagined it as some kind of glamorous transatlantic life. It wasn't that at all, but rather a long-distance family working out how to spend time together. The lives we had built for ourselves, as well as all our intimate friends, were in Gloucester, and we still considered Wellspring House our primary home.

One night when we were away, there was a break-in. After a year with the lights out, the director offered three bedrooms to student interns from nearby Gordon College and Gordon-Conwell Seminary in return for ten hours' work a week. There was no supervision or conversation about what they wanted to learn in their internships at Wellspring. They were to bring their own furniture except for beds and buy their own food and were told not to eat together. We relished breaking that rule—so did they—and sometimes we invited them to sit down with us for supper or ice cream. The young students helped themselves to our lamps or chairs or watched television in our rooms when we weren't there (We never locked the door, so it could be used as a fire exit if necessary). Wellspring felt more like a dorm than a home.

Changes came steadily and quickly after that. Board members did push back. At one point the board made its dissatisfaction known, and the

The Lights Go Out

director decided to step down. But one board member spent a weekend with her and talked her out of resigning. Several board members left when their terms expired. Wellspring had a board of close to twenty people, with two-year terms that could be renewed twice for a total of six years. Several had stayed on longer in order to complete the search, so that a larger number of members than usual were ready to step down at once. The new director cultivated board members from outside Cape Ann, more for their ability to give money than an understanding of Wellspring's culture and our larger community.

The board adopted a new mission statement, focusing on moving program participants toward independence as quickly as possible, rather than teaching them how to take their place in an interdependent community and working toward social change.

For twenty-five years the board had annually renewed its decision to pay local property taxes as a public expression of Wellspring's interdependence with the city and for its services—schools, police, fire, street maintenance, library, and more. The new board voted to get a nonprofit exemption from local taxes.

The City of Gloucester had approached Wellspring House in 2007 about naturalizing the Alewife Creek bordering the property. The channel had been confined by walls, and the city wanted to restore it to a more natural course. That would mean cutting a few small trees and clearing some brush that had grown up on Wellspring's lot. The new director took that opportunity to pave over the vegetable garden and clothesline with a new driveway and parking lot, a highly visible sign of the change in Wellspring's values.

As all of this was happening, an economic recession was shaking the world. Once again, economic hard times made clear that putting the profits of shareholders above public welfare resulted in the huge inequalities that Western nations took for granted. So many people connected with Wellspring—certainly our guests and program participants but also many who came to volunteer or work on the staff—had been victims of those gross inequalities.

Between 2008 and 2010 nine program directors or key staff were fired, and another five resigned. When Steve Carter, the gardener who had loved displaying the beautiful vegetables and flowers he helped grow, was fired, he offered to work for free on the remaining flower beds. His offer was rejected. In a letter the board chair wrote that this loss of staff was "a normal outcome of this period of change."

During the previous economic downturn in 2003, Wellspring staff, program directors, volunteers, and participants were all part of any decisions about organizational changes. Even during the current recession we were witnessing other businesses and nonprofits we knew throughout the community laying the facts on the table and listening to staff ideas about how to survive the economic crisis without layoffs. To keep their jobs, staff often agreed to fewer hours and lower pay in order to ride out the recession. Two program directors at Wellspring wrote letters asking for those kinds of discussions. The letters were not acknowledged, and no such conversations happened.

The recession had a major impact on an affordable-housing project Wellspring was working on at Pond View Village, about a mile away. Back in 2001 Gloucester mayor Bruce Tobey had asked Wellspring to serve as the city's nonprofit partner, and we set up Cape Ann Housing Opportunity to receive grants for the project. It was on a beautiful site that included a former glue factory building that would be rehabilitated overlooking Lower Banjo Pond. The first two phases of affordable units had been completed in 2006: forty-two condos, with a percentage going to first-time homebuyers, and thirty-seven rental units. The project was depending on those sales and rental income to finish the last thirty-five rental units. But with the recession, sales ground to a halt. At the same time a neighboring property owner sued, saying the new apartments would block his units' view. The state Department of Housing and Economic Development had already given $13 million to the project but declined to give any more to finish the last phase until the litigation was settled. The project had to be delayed. The local press was blaming Wellspring, demanding to know what had happened to the state money, insinuating malfeasance. Concerned about potential negative impact on the current fundraising campaign, the director forbade Nancy to speak to a *Boston Globe* reporter who had covered Wellspring for years and wanted to interview her, saying, "Pond View is the worst mistake Wellspring has ever made." A sympathetic local developer stepped in and agreed to finish the project. In the end 114 affordable units went on the market, a very beneficial outcome for the residents of Gloucester, although later than planned. In 2009 the board voted that Wellspring would no longer develop affordable housing.

Many of these changes might be justified in such an economy. Indeed, any new director would be expected to start making changes at some point, even big ones, certainly in an organization run according to a business model. But taken together—along with how the decisions were made— the very heart of Wellspring was ripped out. Our Freirean-based decision-making model of Action/Reflection/Action was done away with. In a matter of months, much of what we had built over twenty-five years was destroyed. It was breathtaking and heartbreaking.

***

In June 2009 the executive committee of the board, including the new director, informed Nancy that her contract as director of legacy projects would not be renewed and asked her to sign a nondisclosure agreement not to discuss Wellspring in the community. A labor lawyer advised Nancy not to sign anything.

Suddenly Nancy had to scramble to get health insurance by the end of the month. She rang Sefatia Romeo Theken, who worked at the local hospital helping low-income people get benefits. Earlier in her life, Sefatia's fisherman husband had lost his boat and committed suicide. During that difficult time for her family, Sefatia had reached out for help and been paired with a Parent Aide. Over the years she, too, had helped many Wellspring families and later became mayor of Gloucester. "Get over here now, and I will see you," Sefatia told Nancy. Within an hour, she had a new insurance policy in place.

The new director and board apparently assumed the two of us would leave Wellspring once Nancy's contract was terminated. They seemed unaware of the founders' lease until we pointed it out. Wellspring was our home. We wanted to stay, though it was clear we were living there on sufferance. We were assigned one shelf in the refrigerator and half a shelf in the pantry for our food. A paid "hospitality coordinator" made lunch for the staff, and we were allowed to join if we signed up. If we wanted to eat breakfast downstairs or do a load of laundry, we had to clear out by 8 a.m. because "Wellspring is a business with business hours." We have to admit, one time Rosemary tossed a pillowcase filled with our laundry down the stairs rather than carrying it, and a couple of our undergarments escaped out onto the floor. A meeting was going on in the adjoining study. We were admonished: Men were there! In our previous life, when Wellspring was a true home to a dozen or more people at a time going about their daily lives, this would have been occasion for much laughter all around and maybe a little teasing and red-faced contrition.

The two of us continued as directors emeritae, attending board meetings. One of our top concerns was the continued exodus of key experienced staff. When staff made suggestions, the director replied, "This is not a democracy." One resigning program director wrote a memo to the board called "What We Have Lost." She said she was experiencing a change of culture, a loss of mutuality at Wellspring, exactly what the Transition Team had said must be preserved.

We wrote the board asking for a discussion with all the lives touched by Wellspring—staff, volunteers, guests, community—about the changes that were coming out of the clash of organizational models: "One is the communitarian one expressed in our mission statement: 'Wellspring is a community of faith, aware that each life touches every other life' ... faith in the basic reality of human beings. Whether we like it or not, we are interdependent ... we are wired for connection. The other organizational model is 'hierarchical-corporate,' where leadership resides in 'the boss'— the executive and the board are the experts; they make the decisions; the workers implement them. In such organizations, there is little or no expectation of consultation with the workers—their questions are discouraged and dissent is not tolerated."

At its summer retreat the board affirmed its commitment to fiscal responsibility, living "within our means," and identifying new community partnerships. There was no reflection on the clash between mutuality and hierarchy. The chair responded to our request in a letter, saying "the board unanimously extended its full support to the executive director and me in our work going forward." We realized that Wellspring was no longer a place where dialogue and disagreement were affirmed as essential to the vitality of the community.

***

Our personal lives and all the meaning they gave us were not dependent on whatever was happening at Wellspring. When you live a life of service, a life of hospitality, you must carve out time and space for your own life and the people in it who sustain you. There will always be weddings, births, deaths, and other joyous and painful milestones. We knew we must make the time to be present, to feel, and to experience each one. The 2010s were brimming over for us, with both joy and sadness.

It's hard to put in words just how thrilling it was to be alive during the successes of the marriage equality movement. Many of us women who loved women never thought we'd ever be able to marry or form civil partnerships and have the same legal rights as heterosexual couples. Marriage had long been the institution where same-sex couples like us were explicitly excluded from the rest of society—socially, culturally, and legally.

Ann Louise and Katherine were way out in front of us and just about everybody. Back in 1982 they celebrated their life commitment in a small private ceremony with a few friends at their house on Cape Ann. A couple of decades later, when they were getting their will and other financial affairs in order in Ireland, their lawyer told them that when one of them died, unlike married people, they would be treated as "strangers in law" when it came to their shared property, pensions, and taxes. That felt wrong.

In 2003 British Columbia opened its doors for gay couples from other countries to marry there, the only place that did. So off to Vancouver they went. When they returned to Ireland, they wrote to the revenue commission to change their tax status from single to married. Katherine—who was an Irish senator at the time, and Ann Louise was a theology professor who served on a state board—still remembers the denial letter they got back, which started "Dear Ladies." They appealed the decision. Many Irish couples go outside the country to get married so, they asked, why wasn't their legal Canadian marriage recognized?

They also gathered feminists and other supporters around their kitchen table to form a group called Marriage Equality, to help fund-raise and strategize their case. One of the group's founders, Gráinne Healy, told the *Irish Independent* that the least she could do was support them: "I thought, 'Jaysus, aren't they very brave?'—in Ireland, you know—to be putting themselves in for what was definitely going to be a trial by fire, and just all of the prurient interest that there would be in these two well-known, very middle-class, middle-aged women coming out as lesbians." Called the KAL case, it made headlines in more than sixty countries but lost at the High Court.

They realized that the only thing that would allow them to live in Ireland as a married couple would be a change to the Irish Constitution. The movement took hold, a national referendum was put on the ballot, and they started campaigning. Katherine and Ann Louise were welcomed by the media and on late-night television spots as the "ideal poster girls" for their warmth, openness, intelligence, and long commitment to each other. In 2015 the referendum passed. On the day it was announced, Katherine took the microphone in front of the celebrating crowd and asked Ann Louise, "Will you marry me in Ireland?" to great cheers. They had changed the Constitution, and Ireland became the first country to say yes to marriage equality by popular vote.

We were much quieter about our relationship. Women of our generation didn't talk much about our love for each other. Of course, our closest friends and some family knew. Nancy told her sister. For Rosemary, it was more complicated. Though Algy had announced their separation long before, they never divorced and remained committed to supporting each other as friends. When Algy was dying in a Scottish hospital in 2008, Rosemary was at his bedside, with his partner and the whole family.

Some time later we were having morning tea, and Nancy raised how important it was for her to have both of our families affirm our relationship. Rosemary agreed. It was time to make our relationship public with a civil partnership. But Rosemary still had uncertainty and concern about how her twelve children, now in their 50s and 60s, would feel. They had their own stories and emotions about their parents' separation and Rosemary's exit from Lothlorien to America. Their reactions to having two parents who went on to be in same-sex relationships varied tremendously.

On a night out at our favorite pub, we first told Rosemary's son Nic and his wife Pauline and asked them to be our witnesses. Nic actually jumped over the table and shouted, "Finally!"

On June 4, 2011, we had a brief but lovely ceremony at the town hall in Halifax, Yorkshire, making public our commitment to each other. We had lived thirty years together sharing a home and our lives with homeless families, more than 500 of them. The officiant told us she had never married a couple so old but felt so good about it. Rosemary was 84, and Nancy was 73. Then in August we hosted a big party for our families and friends. Ann Louise and Katherine brought a whole fresh salmon for dinner, along with potatoes they had dug from their garden in Ireland that morning. We found an electric keyboard for Don Hommen to play for a sing-along and rented out the second floor of the pub. It was an amazing time and such a joy. Our relationship was public and legal.

***

Surgeries in families often seem to come in clusters, and the two of us went through such a period for a couple of years. Like most people, we wanted to recover in our own home as much as possible. In 2013 Nancy had a shoulder replacement and got permission to use a recliner in a downstairs room at Wellspring during her recovery. One night she rang for help to get to the bathroom, but no one came. She ended up on the floor, unable to get up, with her right arm in a sling. She was able to call 911, and a firetruck came. While waiting for the chief in a second truck, Nancy recognized one of the firefighters as the husband of a former Wellspring staff member, and they chatted happily and caught up on the family's news. A couple years later, as she was recovering from surgery for stenosis in her back, the stairs again defeated her, and she got stuck halfway up. Once more the fire service came and helped her up. But with the patient help of a visiting nurse and occupational therapist, and a lot of hard work, Nancy regained her mobility.

Another cluster of events hit us with the full force of grief, starting in 2015. On August 26, Marygrace McCullough died of cancer. Nancy had called her in Iowa, where she and Don were living, every evening for the last year of her life. Three days before she died, Marygrace called the two of us to say, "I love you and thank you for all that we have shared. Take care of each other." In her final days she spent time alone with each of her stepchildren and grandchildren, leaving a legacy of love for them and for Don, whose grief was almost unbearable.

In April 2016 Paul Veronese became ill and died within just a few days, at the flat where he and Mary Jane were living in Pelham, New Hampshire. Even in grief, Mary Jane remained her kind and funny self. That fall we got a call that Mary Jane had died too. These two stalwart and courageous people had done so much to shape Wellspring by their integrity, vision, and generosity.

In June 2017 a call from Katherine in Dublin brought news that Ann Louise had died of complications from a brain hemorrhage. Our hearts were filled with grief as well as gratitude and memories of our friendship of thirty-six years.

In September we very gratefully celebrated our ninetieth and eightieth birthdays at the local bowling club, with family and friends from both sides of the Atlantic. The deejay asked each table to sing along with a song for each decade of our lives—the Beatles' "Yellow Submarine," "Tradition" from *Fiddler On the Roof*, "Let the People Sing" from *Les Miserables* were a few.

One of the most gratifying events for us in this period of celebrations and heartaches was the thirty-fifth anniversary party for Wellspring, which was observed in June 2017. A new garden had been dug behind the house in memory of the founders who had died: Marygrace, Mary Jane and Paul, and Jeanette Richard. Daisies, which were Marygrace's favorite flower, were in bloom.

At the garden dedication the new Wellspring director, who started in that post in 2015, read a poem by the Gloucester sage and poet Vincent Ferrini:

> The suddenness flowers have
> startled the air
> with their fire and others
> as we do with what is ours
> because we are
> the gardeners of each other.

Then we sang together what had become the "Wellspring Song," Cris Williamson's "Song of the Soul":

> Open my eyes that I may see
> Glimpses of truth thou hast for me! ...
> What do you do for a living,
> Are you forgiving,
> Giving shelter? ...
> And you can sing this song
> Why don't you sing along?
> And we can sing for a long, long time!

The singing freed us to turn to one another, as singing so often had at Wellspring celebrations, greeting friends old and new, hugging, crying, and remembering. We felt some restored hope for Wellspring's future, rooted in community and hospitality.

***

In the background of those joyous and sad times, we found ourselves in a strange twilight of uncertainty about our future at Wellspring. We knew that the executive committee of the board was not comfortable with our continuing to live at 302 Essex Avenue.

The day after the thirty-fifth anniversary party the board chair rang and asked us to meet with her the next day to introduce us to the newly elected chair. We were tying up loose ends before flying to visit family in England in two days, but we made time. In the meeting, the chair and chair-elect informed us that in order to return to Wellspring, they were requiring a safety assessment and had booked an appointment for the next day with the head of the occupational therapy department at a local university. The visiting nurse who had worked with Nancy after one of her surgeries had assessed her ability to manage the stairs and given her a safety all-clear six months before. But the board members told us they didn't consider the assessment valid because Nancy and the nurse had become so friendly while working together. We did not fully realize this was the beginning of the process of removing us from Wellspring.

While we were away, we received another call from the board chairs, saying we could not return to Wellspring. They were concerned by the assessment that we were not able to "escape from home safely."

Five former Transition Committee members, who had drawn up the founders' lease in 2008, became our advocates: Patty Doggett, Anne Gifford, Jackie Littlefield, Leslee Shlopak, and Annie Thomas. They went to the executive committee and explained the history and intention of the lease and urged the board to find solutions to assure our home would remain at Wellspring House. We spoke to the therapist who did the assessment. She told us she was sorry if she wasn't clear enough. She believed we *were* safe to live in the house, both day-to-day and in case of an emergency. She had recommended some general safety measures, not just for us but for everyone using the house: a double handrail for the stairs, visible edging on the steps, and better lighting.

The board then agreed we could continue to live at Wellspring after all, but they would require regular safety assessments before we could return from our semiannual family visits. We asked for a date to talk with the Executive Committee and Transition Committee together, but the meeting was postponed repeatedly and never happened.

Before we traveled for Christmas, the same occupational therapist who had assessed us six months before in June met with us again. She again determined we were safe in the house. She mentioned to us that she did not think her conclusions about our safety would change the minds of the Executive Committee about our living at Wellspring and that she thought there was a reason other than safety why they wanted us to leave.

Once we were away, we realized how tired and stressed we felt and how much the whole situation had filled us with sadness and pain. We were profoundly sad, of course, to feel forced out of the home we had created and loved. But what was most painful was knowing we could have no part in any conversations or decisions about it. We were told several times: "The board will make the decision." During one of our times away, we received a letter that used a phrase from the original mission statement: "*In the spirit of hospitality,* we wish we could continue to offer the house at 302 Essex Avenue to you to stay without reservation or concern as we have for the last ten years." That stung.

The board met in early January 2018, while we were still away, and voted unanimously not to extend the founders' lease. We could come back for one final two-week stay, during which we must move our personal belongings out of the house. The chair e-mailed us the board's vote, followed by a registered letter.

The entire process felt like a manifestation of "Power Over," which avoids dialogue, devalues personal relationships, and sometimes conceals its real goals. We had spent our careers and lives creating a different way of working, living, and being in community and in friendship with others that we called "Power With." Now at the end of our careers, we felt that work had been destroyed, and that our own future was being determined for us in a "Power Over" process. Our feelings of hurt and loss were not only for ourselves. We were profoundly aware of the sadness of so many others for whom Wellspring had been a life-changing experience and who had given so much work and love to create it in the spirit of "Power With." That broke our hearts.

Our friends on the Transition Committee felt we needed to inform a broader group of people that Wellspring's board had voted to terminate the founders' lease, evicting us. Some were so distressed they wanted to go to the press. We did not want that. We wanted to let our friends and community know in our own way, and we didn't want to harm Wellspring. Some wanted us to sue the board for breaking the founders' lease. Our lawyer's opinion was that we would win, but we felt the bad feeling of a lawsuit would do more harm than good, to all of us. In the end, the Transition Committee shared the news in a letter to Wellspring's many friends and supporters.

***

Now we had lost our home. We did not know where we would live. When the seven founders started Wellspring, we each agreed to contribute monthly to a budget that would help pay off our two mortgages and cover other expenses. We called that "rent," solely because it helped us gain charitable tax status for Wellspring donors. None of us were thinking about retirement or home equity. Over our years at Wellspring, we calculated, the two of us contributed about a quarter of a million dollars. Once we founders paid off the two mortgages on Wellspring House, we could never have imagined this unfolding of events.

Back in 1991, when we conducted research with our formerly homeless guests for "We Are Like You," we got a clear message that now resonated with us: At the moment we were forced to leave one housing situation, just as they had, we were having trouble finding another one we could afford on our retirement income, which was mostly Social Security benefits. Gloucester had dramatically gentrified. Both rents and real estate values had soared since we had bought Wellspring House for $140,000. It was now appraised at more than $1 million.

Yet we had resources, largely in the generosity and support of a community that believed in mutuality. Our advocates on the Transition Committee helped us set up a fund at a local bank, where community members could contribute donations to help us with housing expenses. Once we no longer needed assistance, any remaining funds would go to a North Shore organization to develop and manage affordable housing.

The hardest part was finding somewhere to live in Gloucester. Friends helped us look but were coming up empty. Then we learned that Annie Thomas's daughter and her husband, who were living and working in western Massachusetts, had recently bought a small house in West Gloucester to fix up so they could vacation near family. They proposed we rent it, and we could coordinate our visits to family in England with theirs to Gloucester. They pushed ahead with the rehab work—floors, paint, electric outlets—working all hours to get it ready by the time we had to be out of Wellspring. The house had very little furniture, so we were able to bring ours, which they could use too.

We still had to dispose of much of our personal and work-related possessions in just two weeks, including our library of beloved books. Donna Haig Friedman organized the move for us. There was a "parcel day," when we mailed books and other items family and friends wanted. We gave the books on social justice and feminism to a college in New Hampshire and the rest to Gloucester's Sawyer Free Library, which would add them to their collection or sell them to raise funds. We were greatly relieved they would be put to good use.

On moving day a team of volunteers gathered into the two rooms we had occupied for thirty-five years, briskly packing, labeling, carrying, and at our insistence taking items they could use, then driving, unpacking, and even making our bed up in our new rented home. There was a strong feeling of energy and camaraderie as the work progressed, though everyone understood the sadness that underlay all the activity. The image of our two bare rooms—our lives and memories moved out, all swept clean—will stay with us always.

***

The story of a rocky founder-successor transition is not an unusual one. In the beginning of so many organizations, especially mission-driven ones, there are the passionate founders, who will work any hours, and do things like vacuum the living room, welcome back a former guest to be cared for in her dying moments, try new ideas, and bring all they've got to make their vision succeed. When it's time for them to step aside, their successors often seek to restructure and take the organization more into the mainstream. Transitioning from a founder to a second director is extraordinarily challenging. Many organizations don't survive it.

There's another story at work here, which is not an unusual one either: Almost all of us who live long enough to retire will see our capacities diminish—physically, mentally, often both. Those coming up behind us in our families, homes, and work must balance respect, compassion, and safety, while living their own dreams. It's messy and can be painful, even with the best of intentions. Western culture doesn't have a good model of how to care for, respect, and value the wisdom of our elders.

Both of these are archetypal stories.

But we had created something that was not at all usual or archetypal. Wellspring was our home, our work, and our community, all in one. That was true for many of the lives it touched. We deliberately blurred those and many other boundaries. Wellspring was committed above all to social change. That was what we wanted, and those years were the most fulfilling of our lives. In seeking to offer radical hospitality, we created a place that aspired to be a community, a home, a workplace, a service, and a social-change agent, all at once.

All of us went into the transition with our eyes wide open. We spent much time with talented organizational experts who really understood us, we brought our Action/Reflection practice to the task, and we worked very deliberately with a Transition Team over two years.

Where we were naïve was believing that we had created a community that had practiced mutuality for so long that habit would continue after we had stepped down.

Where we were blindsided was not realizing how fragile our organization was; how vulnerable it was to anyone who wanted "Power Over"; and how much it depended on mutual trust, not a board resolution, notarized certificate, or lease.

What was painful was that when we were the ones in need, we had no say in the decisions made about us, after the lengths we had gone to make sure every voice was heard.

What was excruciatingly ironic was that after decades of serving homeless women, we were forced to leave our home without knowing if we could find another we could afford. And we were completely unprepared for that.

We still believe we are all one family, as Phyllis Fireman told us years before. Becoming homeless could happen to any of us, at any point. We expected when we were no longer the ones doing the work, our community would carry it on and "cart our asses" around Gloucester, if need be, as Ellen had said to Mary Jane. Our community—the people who worked, volunteered, and were served by Wellspring—did step up in many ways to do exactly that and care for us personally. But in the end, none of us could safeguard the values of mutuality and social change of Wellspring the organization. The institutional forces, the nonprofit structure, the grant and government agency requirements, the money, were too strong.

Since our moving day in 2018, we have reflected on these events a lot. Some of our mistakes and blind spots were particular to Wellspring. Those may be cautionary for the next generation who want to change their lives and create a new kind of organization and new ways to work together for a more just society. Some of our reflections have more to do with needed structural changes, also a job for the next generation.

So many of the resources available to nonprofits for succession planning fit a cookie-cutter model. Nonprofits have increasingly taken on a capitalistic business model, with power from the top and a strong emphasis on money over mission. So much time and effort is expended on fundraising and competing for grants. The consultant we hired was steeped in that model.

When our own Transition Team looked at handbooks for the transition, they got distracted by lesser questions like: How will you let the public know? What should the news releases say? Who's on your mailing list? What if the founder dies before a successor is found? There's a crying need for better structures and advice for communitarian organizations like ours.

At one point the Search Committee, including the two of us, met with our close sister organization, Project Hope Boston, and deputy director Dan Curley advised us: "This is your organization. You can do what you want in this process. You're entitled to that. Hold on to that. Don't let it go." That voice is sorely needed in the conversation.

The Search Committee and board should not have stuck with a consultant who didn't agree with what all of us wanted. When our first offer to a candidate didn't work out, we should have seized that moment to discontinue the relationship. Yet the organization had already spent so much on the contract. The board decided to stay the course and just keep arguing.

We moved too fast. After the first offer didn't land a candidate, we should have taken a pause. We should have looked for an interim director. In fact, two employees did offer to serve as interim codirectors. We could have hired a coach for them.

Or we could have reorganized the way our colleague Meg Wheatley did. Meg founded Berkana Institute to consult with and coach women in many countries on leadership models that engage rather than dominate. Despite that mission, Meg saw her organization sliding into the conventional hierarchical nonprofit mold after she stepped down. She stepped right back in, streamlined the staff and board, and now oversees an army of volunteers to keep the mission going.

Our team relied too much on the assumption that an internal candidate understood the mission and culture. Reflecting now, we should have given more weight to the fact she had just completed an MBA and brought that mindset, where top-down management and "Power Over" are the default. The Search Committee didn't ask how candidates would carry the core values of mutuality and Action/Reflection into a future vision. There was nothing about our self-organizing processes in the job description.

At a critical, vulnerable moment, Wellspring lost institutional memory on our board. Terms expired, and key leaders stepped off. Years before, we had set a policy of term limits, thinking we wanted to constantly bring in new perspectives, mentor new board members, and create a deep bench of leadership. That worked while long-term directors and staff held on to the institution's memory. We did not foresee how quickly a board could be wholly remade by giving those seats to donors, which is the default in the nonprofit world.

We question now whether a communitarian organization style and mutuality work once you get past a certain size. Mutuality requires personal contact.

By taking state contracts and grants, we had unwittingly signed up for parts of the conventional nonprofit structure. If we had never taken that funding, could we have stayed closer to our values? Perhaps. But we would have had less impact. We would have had to stick to doing one thing well, such as running a shelter.

When you apply for public funding and grants, those agencies and foundations want to see your list of board members and organizational chart. The board is assumed to be the long-term owner and makes the big decisions, and the founder or director reports to it. We can imagine a world where local and state governments are pushed for policies that give more flexibility with visionary organizational models. What if communitarian organizations convened a small board, three to five people, just for the purpose of grants and fund-raising, then an advisory group for running the organization? We urge the rising generation of mission-driven visionaries to look at our mistakes and rethink the whole idea of nonprofit governance structures.

In 1980 we wanted to change our lives. We wanted to create a home and offer hospitality to people who needed a home for a while. We immersed ourselves in touching what it meant to be human, to be connected, and to be mutual. That came to seem natural. We never understood how radical we were.

Epilogue: The Power of Mutuality

It's been six years since we moved out of Wellspring House. We have increasingly made our home in England, especially during the pandemic years. We still spend lots of time with our families and friends in both America and in England, sharing with them joys and tragedies and changes. And we've written this book. Hundreds of people were part of Wellspring's story. We've continued to be in touch with many of them, and some have continued to meet and to remember with us. And they urged us to write that story down.

Just a few months after we were evicted from Wellspring, we were invited to talk about our experience at Gloucester's new Writers' Center. Back in 2010 Annie Thomas—someone who came to us as a young mother looking to volunteer and came to embody all that Wellspring was—had gotten a call to help save the little house on East Main Street where Gloucester's poet laureate Vincent Ferrini had lived, written, and mentored other writers. Vincent, who had grown up in poverty himself, always believed in the talents of people in poverty. Annie did, too. She embraced the Freirean model, and she also believed in the motto Ann Louise Gilligan had instilled in us: If you can imagine it, you can do it. Within weeks she and Vincent's nephew, Henry, had raised the money to establish a writers' center where the working-class people of the city could tell their stories. Some met in weekly groups. Writers were invited to stay free for a week at a time, to write in the one-room house lined with bookshelves. For many it was the first time they had told their stories. When we attended the center's opening event, a Korean War veteran, tears streaming down his face, told the heart-breaking story of being a young man thrust into war and how he never got warm the whole time he was there.

Our own talk there was also the first time we had told our story publicly. Many people who came to listen had been part of it. Some wept, but most of all they wanted the story to be told. Write it! they said. Let it have a chance to be known and to go on, inspiring others.

We began to plan out the chapters and gather and sort the material we had managed to save: event programs and fund-raising brochures, letters from the board and from friends, newspaper articles about how we got started, about big occasions and celebrations, protests and social movements and demonstrations in which we had taken part. The amount of material was daunting, but we were excited. We realized that though our work at Wellspring was over, the story could still change lives.

A readers group gathered around the project, encouraging us to believe the job was worth doing: Donna and Steve Friedman, Katherine Zappone, and Chuck Collins. They were all convinced of the importance of the book, but they all said, "You need an editor!" The one we found was Kimberly French, whose skill and experience pushed the whole project into a new place of a writing partnership. Regular Zoom meetings with her and with the readers group helped us through some tough times, when illness and age discouraged us and slowed us down. We kept going, and Chuck and Kimberly worked on book proposals to send to prospective publishers.

***

We want to conclude our conversation with our readers with a few final stories that carry on the power of mutuality—the skills, the organizational imagination, endurance, and energy that are released when determined people gather to achieve a group purpose. And we wanted to introduce a new framework that could help readers think and imagine in a new way, a way of thought that is transforming the way scientists think, particularly the way we assign importance.

What we most want readers of this book and aspiring activists to know is this: In order to practice mutuality, you don't have to start a whole new organization the way Annie and Henry did with the Gloucester Writers Center, Katherine and Ann Louise did with An Cosán, and we did with Wellspring. Mutuality can be practiced in a new organization, in an existing one, or as an individual. After Cape Ann Families was closed in 2010 and Stacy Randell was fired as program director, Stacy got a job at North Shore Community College, which operated on a typical top-down model. Stacy was so grounded in the principles of mutuality, working cooperatively, and listening deeply, and she wanted to bring those principles to the college. Her bosses were not used to getting feedback, but Stacy kept asking students and people in the community what they most needed. In response, she created an Adult Learning Center within her department, where students from the community could come for free literacy classes, job training, and preparation for their GED or high school equivalency test (HiSET). Classes are small, and students can progress at their own pace. All staff and students are asked to contribute their reflections on how the program is going in a journal. If a student has difficulties, teachers will look for hands-on or other approaches rather than conventional lectures and text. When someone passes a subject test, they celebrate. When you walk onto the fourth floor where the center is located, the whole ambience, with its banners and flowers, tells you something is different about this place. And that's because of Stacy's persistence and commitment to mutuality.

Similarly, one of our original founders, Sissy LaVoie, has held on to her experience with mutuality and hospitality and re-created it in her own home in northwest Florida. She and her husband, Mark, have taken in many women, young and old, in despair, some homeless, some depressed, even a 54-year-old neighbor addicted to prescription drugs. Some young women who came to them felt they had nowhere to turn until they could finish their schooling or re-establish a relationship with their families. Mark and Sissy have used their experience in the real-estate business to advise people who are in danger of foreclosure on how to save their homes. Whenever a hurricane is forecast, they open their home to up to five families whose homes are in the projected pathway, including their pets. "Sometimes to help someone," Sissy says, "all you need to do is just listen and hear them, offer your time, just believe in them, and let them know they are not alone."

***

Fordhall Farm is a 140-acre farm in the English midlands near the Welsh border, run by sister and brother Charlotte and Ben Hollins. Bounded by a river and a main road, it consists of pasture, woodland, and several farm buildings. The farm sells its meat, eggs, honey, preserves, and other produce at its own farm shop, cafe, and vans at sporting events. Underpinning it all is the skillfully nurtured land that makes all this possible and that was nearly lost forever.

When Charlotte had just graduated from university and Ben was only 18, they were threatened with losing not just their home but their way of life. Their father, Arthur, was a sick man, worn out from years of struggle to make the farm viable. Their mother, Connie, was deeply depressed. Prospective developers were pressuring the landowner. The farm was not able to pay its rent, and the owner had no choice but to evict the Hollins family. Angry and miserable, they argued, contradicted each other, tried to accept the inevitable, struggling for months to keep going what was left of the stock. Sympathetic, the landlord gave them eighteen more months. Charlotte and Ben set out to raise the impossible sum of £800,000 to buy the land. Their infectious conviction that their home and their dream should be saved convinced others, too. Charlotte and a small team of fellow believers went door to door, wrote articles, distributed leaflets, gave talks on nationwide radio. They spread the word about the natural outdoor-grazing system called *foggage farming* that Arthur had developed after World War II, rotating the stock from the wetland meadows in summer to the sandy hills in winter. It was a way to reduce the farm's reliance on costly grains and oil-based inputs and to produce 100 percent grass-fed meat.

Money came in but much too slowly, as the days raced by. The drama of their struggle touched people, who also caught the spirit of why this bit of land mattered, not just for those directly involved but for the future of farming and food and for a whole community. Not till the last day did they know if they would have enough to buy the land. Even once they achieved their goal, that was still just the beginning. The same spirit has helped Fordhall rebuild and regrow. Its hospitality attracts hundreds of volunteers, including people with physical and mental disabilities, who take on dozens of roles, educating, inspiring, digging, building, learning, hosting events and holiday weekends in yurts, creating nature trails. And the ideas keep coming.

So much about Fordhall makes us think of the early days of Wellspring. It is a product of the same kind of commitment the Wellspring founders had, right down to Action/Reflection. The diverse board and the shareholders don't take a next step without reflecting on the farm's mission. Because it is both a home and serves a mission, it needed a unique structure. The Fordhall Community Land Initiative has one farmer (Ben didn't want a committee running the farm) and 8,000 shareholders. We are proud to be among those 8,000 who caught the spirit of why this land mattered and the hope it has brought to a community.

***

In our latter Wellspring years, we got to know another, older organization called ATD Fourth World, which continues to inspire us. In 1956 a young priest, Father Joseph Wresinski, was assigned to be a chaplain to 250 homeless people living in an emergency camp near Paris. They were living crowded in Quonset huts on a muddy field with just four spigots of water. Wresinski, who himself was born in a detainment camp during World War II, was shocked by the extreme poverty and squalor he encountered. He was moved to make this promise: These families will climb the steps to the presidential palace in France, the Vatican, and the United Nations.

The next year he created Aide à Toute Detresse (ATD or Help for All in Distress; in English, the organization uses the acronym to stand for All Together in Dignity). French people stepped up to help, becoming the foundation of the ATD Volunteer Corps. Their method was not to hand out aid, but to work alongside people living in poverty and to listen to their stories of what they had experienced and their ideas of what they needed. The volunteers often started with a street library. They would gather the children, read them stories, and give them books. That got the parents' interest. They started having conversations, asking, just as Paulo Freire did: Why are you in poverty? What do you need? In that first camp, alongside the parents, they created a kindergarten, library, chapel, laundry, workshop, and beauty parlor. People who came out of extreme poverty were always at the center of the organization's leadership. Their ideas were considered just as important as any coming from an academic or aid organization, even more so.

Over the years Father Wresinski's promise was fulfilled. In 1987 more than 100,000 people gathered on Plaza of Liberties and Human Rights in Paris to dedicate a stone honoring the victims of poverty, inscribed: "Wherever Men and Women are condemned to live in extreme poverty, human rights are violated. To come together to ensure that these rights are respected is our solemn duty." Two years after that, more than

300 delegates from families living in extreme poverty climbed the steps of the Vatican to meet with Pope John Paul II. Then in 1992 the United Nations General Assembly declared October 17 International Day for the Eradication of Poverty, which has been observed every year since, with men and women from the ATD Fourth World climbing the steps of the United Nations. ATD Fourth World now works in thirty-two countries on five continents, including six areas of the United States, "bringing together people from all walks of life, learning from people who face poverty every day and running family and community projects."

Fourth World volunteer Susie Devins introduced us to this work, when she was a visiting fellow at the Center for Social Policy at the University of Massachusetts in Boston, directed by our close friend and colleague Donna Haig Friedman. Since 2010 Susie and Donna have cofacilitated ATD Fourth World groups and retreats, in particular on peace building and on violence done to people who are poor. We attended one of their retreats, with people from New York City, post-Katrina New Orleans, and from Boston reading their own stories of shame, abuse, and the day-to-day struggles to survive. As at Wellspring, we saw once again that it is the people in poverty who know best what they need and are the best evaluators of the effectiveness of the professional helpers.

***

The last story we want to tell is about fungi, an astonishing organism that most people notice only by its "fruit," which can just appear overnight, in all kinds of ecosystems all over the world, in a huge range of forms, colors, and sizes. Sometimes it disappears the next day. But as an organism, it travels continuously underground, as almost invisible threads, seeking food, finding a way around obstacles, exchanging nutrients with plants, sometimes creating huge mats, swallowing up and digesting other organisms it meets.

We've been captivated by the work of Merlin Sheldrake in his book *Entangled Life: How Fungi Make Our Worlds, Change Our Minds & Shape Our Futures*. Scientists' growing understanding of fungi both gives us a metaphor of how to understand human communities and may even teach us how to make better decisions and impact how we behave.

One example is slime molds. These are creatures that have no brain or central nervous system yet make decisions all the time by comparing possible courses of action and finding the shortest path. In experiments, these molds have found the most efficient route in models that have closely mirrored the same routes humans developed for Tokyo's rail system and the Roman roads of central Europe.

More than 90 percent of plants depend on fungi in some way, a relationship that was initially called "symbiosis" in the nineteenth century. But with more study of fungi, some scientists are describing some of those relationships as "mutualism." By growing within the roots of plants, which makes sugar and lipids through photosynthesis, fungi get fed. For their part, fungi are terrific foragers and can scavenge water and minerals underground that feed the plant. They must cooperate because each needs the other. Fungi have even been shown to "reward" more cooperative plant partners—for example, supplying them more of the necessary carbon and phosphorus that they need to grow.

One application of fungi holds unexpected hope for our world. Solid forms of fungi can learn to fill spaces prepared for them, forming walls or even buildings, creating protected spaces for displaced or homeless people or for storage of supplies, for as long as needed. Yet they are degradable when not needed, leaving no residue. Another application is in the fast-growing field of biocomputing. Fungi could use electrical signaling as a basis for rapid communication and serve as large-scale environmental sensors, for example, reporting changes in soil quality, water purity, pollution, or other hazards.

More far reaching is what this phenomenon does to our thinking. An organization called Radical Mycology argues that a better understanding of fungi has the power to change the way we think and imagine. It forces us to ask disturbing and revolutionary new questions: Where do we stand in the hierarchy of intelligence? How different would our organizations and communities look if we held up the mutualistic behavior of fungi as a typical model of life forms, rather than competition, hierarchy, predation, parasitism, and survival of the fittest?

This can still sound very theoretical, but in practical terms it has to be at the heart of our understanding of mutuality, community, collaboration,

Freirean cycles of reflection and decision making. The threads of discovery, sharing, deciding and exchanging, move steadily and inexorably under our feet and in our meetings and erupt into new fruit (and forms) and release more spores (and ideas).

We see in all these stories reasons for hope. In a time when disasters, natural and human made, can fill us with despair, we must lift up all these threads of courage and compassion that keep pushing their way from darkness to light, drawing on unknown reserves of ingenuity, and bursting out in unstoppable newness and hope.

This book is the contribution of Nancy and Rosemary, and of Kimberly and all the people you have met in it and many others too, to making sure you notice what is going on and still growing. After we notice it, we all need to talk and reflect, then become part of it, by active engagement, but also by changing our ways of thinking and dreaming and living. We will see you farther down the road, underground or over.

Bibliography

Introduction: Evicted

The Editors, "Executive Leadership Transition: What We Know," *Nonprofit Quarterly,* December 21, 2002, <https://nonprofitquarterly.org/executive-leadership-transition-what-we-know/>

"The Nonprofit Leadership Development Deficit," Nonprofit CEO Transitions Resource Center, The Bridgespan Group, July 14, 2016, <https://www.bridgespan.org/insights/nonprofit-ceo-transitions-resource-center>

Chapter 1: Change Your Life

Pope Paul VI, "Documents of the Second Vatican Council," November 18, 1965, <https://www.vatican.va/archive/hist_councils/ii_vatican_council/documents/vat-ii_const_19651118_dei-verbum_en.html>

Chapter 2: Loving and Living

Freire, Paulo, *Pedagogy of the Oppressed* (New York: Seabury Press, 1970).

Haughton, Rosemary, "Freedom and the Individual," in *Objections to Roman Catholicism,* edited by Michael de la Bédoyère (Philadelphia: Lippincott, 1965).

Haughton, Rosemary, *The Transformation of Man: A Study of Conversion and Community* (London: Geoffrey Chapman, 1967).

Haughton, Rosemary, *Tales from Eternity: The World of Fairytales and the Spiritual Search* (New York: Seabury Press, 1973).

Chapter 3: Finding a Home

Becket, Ed, "Stories in Time: Museum Looks Back at Native Americans of Cape Ann," *Wicked Local*, October 16, 2020, <https://www.wickedlocal.com/story/cape-ann-beacon/2020/10/16/opinion-native-americans-of-cape-ann/42960531/>

Dreier, Peter, "Reagan's Legacy: Homelessness in America," *Shelterforce*, May 1, 2004, <https://shelterforce.org/2004/05/01/reagans-legacy-homelessness-in-america/>

"History of Cape Ann," Cape Ann Museum, <https://www.capeannmuseum.org/about/history-of-the-museum/history-of-cape-ann/>

Hyer, Marjorie, "Massachusetts Town Mobilizes against Moonies," *Washington Post*, August 25, 1980, <https://www.washingtonpost.com/archive/politics/1980/08/25/massachusetts-town-mobilizes-against-moonies/>

Jones, Marian Moser, "Creating a Science of Homelessness during the Reagan Era," *Milbank Quarterly* (March 5, 2015), 139–78, <https://ncbi.nlm.nih.gov/pmc/articles/PMC4364434/>

Law, Claire, "A Wellspring of Black Family History Uncovered at Gloucester House," *Boston Globe*, June 19, 2023, <https://www.bostonglobe.com/2023/06/19/metro/wellspring-black-family-history-uncovered-gloucester-house>

National Academies of Sciences, Engineering, and Medicine, "The History of Homelessness in the United States," in *Permanent Supportive Housing: Evaluating the Evidence for Improving Health Outcomes among People Experiencing Chronic Homelessness* (Washington, DC: The National Academies Press, 2018), <https://doi.org/10.17226/25133>

Native Land Map, Douglas D. Schumann Library & Learning Commons, Wentworth Institute of Technology, updated Fall 2023, <https://library.wit.edu/guides/native-american-heritage>

Roth, Alisa, "The Truth about Deinstitutionalization," *The Atlantic*, May 25, 2021, <https://www.theatlantic.com/health/archive/2021/05/truth-about-deinstitutionalization/618986/>

SFWeekly Staff, "The Great Eliminator: How Ronald Reagan Made Homelessness Permanent," *SFWeekly*, June 29, 2016, <https://www.sfweekly.com/archives/

the-great-eliminator-how-ronald-reagan-made-homelessness-permanent/article_92c9b2ac-e881-502a-ae9d-5266cac03404.html>

Special to the *New York Times*, "Gloucester's Alarm at Moon's Church Abates," *New York Times*, January 9, 1984, Section D, Page 12, <https://www.nytimes.com/1984/01/09/us/gloucester-s-alarm-at-moon-s-church-abates.html>

Chapter 4: Homemaking

Bass, Alison, "A Wellspring of Caring," *Boston Globe*, April 5, 1999, E1–E5.

Furlong, Monica, *The New Women Included: Book of Services and Prayers* (London: SPCK, Society for Promoting Christian Knowledge, 1996).

Haughton, Rosemary, *Song in a Strange Land: The Wellspring Story and the Homelessness of Women* (Springfield, IL: Templegate, 1990).

Haughton, Rosemary, *The Catholic Thing* (Springfield, IL: Templegate, 1994).

Zappone, Katherine, and Ann Louise Gilligan, *Our Lives Out Loud* (Dublin: O'Brien Press, 2008).

Chapter 5: Stretching Hospitality

Bassuk, Ellen L., Lenore Rubin, and Alison Lauriat, "Is Homelessness a Mental-Health Problem?," *American Journal of Psychiatry* 141, no. 12 (December 1984), 1546–50.

Bassuk, Ellen L. and Lynn Rosenburg, "The Psychosocial Characteristics of Homeless and Housed Children," *Pediatrics* 85, no. 3 (March 1990), 257–61.

Bogard, Cynthia J., J. Jeff McConnell, Naomi Gerstel, and Michael Schwartz, "Homeless Mothers and Depression: Misdirected Policy," *Journal of Health and Social Behavior*, 40, no. 1 (March 1999), 46–62.

Egan, Timothy, "Hook, Line and Sunk," *The New York Times Magazine*, December 11, 1994, Section 6, page 75, <https://www.nytimes.com/1994/12/11/magazine/hook-line-and-sunk.html>

Gateley, Edwina, *God Goes to Church* (Trabuco Canyon, CA: Source Books; Erie, PA: Pax Christi USA Publications, Copublishers, 1999).

Gateley, Edwina, *In God's Womb: A Spiritual Memoir* (Maryknoll, NY: Orbis Books, 2009).

Hillinger, Charles, "Gloucester Hangs Out 'Gone Fishin' Sign," *Los Angeles Times*, October 14, 1990, <https://www.latimes.com/archives/la-xpm-1990-10-14-vw-3328-story.html>

"Lena Mary Parisi Novello 1917–2005," Gloucester 400 Stories Project, 2023, <https://gloucesterma400.org/wp-content/uploads/400-Stories-Project-Lena-Novello.pdf>

Murawski, Steven A., "A Brief History of the Groundfishing Industry of New England," *History of NOAA Fisheries in the Northeast*, <https://www.fisheries.noaa.gov/new-england-mid-atlantic/commercial-fishing/brief-history-groundfishing-industry-new-england#period-6.-too-many-fishermen...-chasing-too-few-fish-(1985-1995)>

Ricard, C. J., *The Resurrection Plant: Your Pain Is Your Path to Greatness* (Powell, OH: Author Academy Elite, 2021).

Vogt, Amanda, "Fixing the Original Sin," *Chicago Tribune*, April 10, 1994, <https://www.chicagotribune.com/1994/04/10/fixing-the-original-sin/>

Chapter 6: Housing Should Be a Right

Clendinen, Dudley, "Dukakis, at Inauguration, Vows to Aid Needy in Massachusetts," *New York Times*, January 7, 1983, <https://www.nytimes.com/1983/01/07/us/dukakis-at-inauguration-vows-to-aid-needy-in-massachusetts.html>

Collins, Chuck, *Born on Third Base: A One Percenter Makes the Case for Tackling Inequality, Bringing Wealth Home, and Committing to the Common Good* (White River Junction, VT: Chelsea Green Publishing, 2016).

Emanuel, Gabrielle, "State-Funded Shelters in Massachusetts Reach New Record: Nearly 5,000 Families," *WBUR Radio*, July 25, 2023, <https://www.wbur.org/news/2023/07/25/family-homelessness-record-high>

"Forty Facts about Habitat and Housing," Habitat for Humanity, <https://www.habitat.org/stories/40-facts-about-habitat-humanity-and-housing>

French, Kimberly, "From Riches to Responsibility," *UU World*, March/April 2003, <https://www.uuworld.org/articles/riches-responsibility>

Gross, Samantha J., "Boston Civil Rights Group Sues State over Plan to Set Limits on Right-to-Shelter Law," *Boston Globe*, October 27, 2023, <https://www.bost

onglobe.com/2023/10/27/metro/migrant-crisis-lawsuit-healey-emergency-response-shelter-law/>

Gross, Samantha J., "In Massachusetts Race to Shelter Homeless Families, Some Local Governments Balk," *Boston Globe*, May 5, 2023, <https://www.bostonglobe.com/2023/05/03/metro/mass-race-shelter-homeless-families-some-local-governments-balk-state-is-moving-change-that/>

Roosevelt, Franklin D., "Inaugural Address," American Presidency Project, University of California at Santa Barbara, January 20, 1937, <https://shelterforce.org/2004/05/01/reagans-legacy-homelessness-in-america/>

Roosevelt, Franklin D., "Inaugural Address," American Presidency Project, University of California at Santa Barbara, January 20, 1945, <https://www.presidency.ucsb.edu/documents/inaugural-address-6>

Rothstein, Richard, *The Color of Law: A Forgotten History of How Our Government Segregated America* (New York: Liveright Publishing Corporation, 2017).

Sirgany, Adam, "Remembering Mitch Snyder," *National Coalition for the Homeless News*, July 2010, <https://nationalhomeless.org/news/RememberingMitchSnyder.html>

Tars, Eric, "Housing as a Human Right," 2018 Advocates' Guide, National Low Income Housing Coalition, <https://nlihc.org/sites/default/files/AG-2018/Ch01-S06_Housing-Human-Right_2018.pdf>

"Urban Renewal and the Fitz Henry Lane House," Cape Ann Museum, <https://artsandculture.google.com/story/urban-renewal-and-the-fitz-henry-lane-house-cape-ann-museum/AQVhbGPbOIKoKA?hl=en>

von Hoffman, Alexander, "History Lessons for Today's Housing Policy," Joint Center for Housing Studies, Harvard University, August 2012, <https://jchs.harvard.edu/sites/default/files/w12-5_von_hoffman.pdf>

Chapter 7: Celebration

Dalai Lama and Desmond Tutu, with Douglas Abrams, *The Book of Joy: Lasting Happiness in a Changing World* (Hot Springs Village, AR: Cornerstone Publishers, 2016).

Johnson, Karan, "The Surprising Power of Daily Rituals," *BBC*, February 24, 2022, <https://www.bbc.com/future/article/20210914-how-rituals-help-us-to-deal-with-uncertainty-and-stress>

Nichols, T., and C. Jacques, "Family Reunions: Communities Celebrate New Possibilities," in *The Reflecting Team in Action: Collaborative Practice in Family Therapy*, edited by Steven Friedman (New York: Guilford Press, 1995).

Chapter 8: What Is Radical Hospitality?

Friedman, Donna Haig, *Parenting in Public: Family Shelter and Public Assistance* (New York: Columbia University Press, 2000).
Hemminger, Helen, "We Are Like You," in *Choosing the Future I, Proceedings of a Symposium*, Gloucester, MA, May 31–June 1, 1991.
Leonard, Margaret A., and Stacy Randell, "Policy Shifts in the Massachusetts Response to Family Homelessness," *New England Journal of Public Policy* 8, Issue 1, Article 42, <https://scholarworks.umb.edu/nejpp/vol8/iss1/42/>
Quinones, Wendy, "Let Them Have Housing," *New England Journal of Public Policy* 8, Issue 1, Article 50, 557–81, <https://scholarworks.umb.edu/nejpp/vol8/iss1/50/>

Chapter 9: Education Is the Key

Belenkey, Mary Field, Blythe Mcvicker Clinchy, Nancy Rule Goldberger, and Jill Mattuck Tarule, *Women's Ways of Knowing: The Development of Self, Voice, and Mind* (New York: Basic Books, 1986).
"Boston Women's Memorial," City of Boston, <https://www.boston.gov/departments/womens-advancement/boston-womens-memorial>
Díaz, Kim, "Paulo Freire (1921-1997)," Internet Encyclopedia of Philosophy, A Peer-Reviewed Academic Resource, <https://iep.utm.edu/Freire/>
Haughton, Rosemary, and Nancy Schwoyer, "Welfare Reform and National Scapegoating: The Politics of Fear," *Cross Currents* (Spring 1995), Volume 45, 80–94.
Hayward, Nancy, "Susan B. Anthony," National Women's History Museum, 2017, <https://www.womenshistory.org/education-resources/biographies/susan-brownell-anthony>

Irigaray, Luce, *Speculum of the Other Woman* (Ithaca, New York: Cornell University Press, 1985).
Matthews, Dylan, "'If the Goal Was to Get Rid of Poverty, We Failed': The Legacy of the 1996 Welfare Reform," *Vox,* June 20, 2016, <https://www.vox.com/2016/6/20/11789988/clintons-welfare-reform>
Waring, Marilyn, *If Women Counted: A New Feminist Economics* (New York: Harper & Row, 1988).
"Women's Activism in Lowell," Lowell National Historical Park, National Park Service, <https://www.nps.gov/lowe/learn/historyculture/womensactivism.htm>
Zappone, Katherine, and Ann Louise Gilligan, *Love and Social Change* (Dublin: An Cosán, 2006).

Chapter 10: A Community Ecosystem

"Angela Sanfilippo Named to Boston Seafood Hall of Fame," *Commercial Fisheries News,* September 2016, <https://fish-news.com/cfn/angela-sanfilippo-named-to-boston-seafood-hall-of-fame/>
Horgan, Sean, "Fighting for Fishing Grounds in Face of Wind Farms," *Gloucester Daily Times*, June 1, 2021, <https://www.gloucestertimes.com/news/fishing_industry_news/fighting-for-fishing-grounds-in-face-of-wind-farms/article_1add69c8-7baf-5085-8042-6259b1145620.html>
Horgan, Sean, "Fisherman's Wife Named to Seafood Hall of Fame," *Gloucester Daily Times,* August 3, 2016, <gloucestertimes.com/news/fishing_industry_news/fisherman-s-wife-named-to-seafood-hall-of-fame/article_8907c01a-4410-5593-a1aa-55da170ff90b.html>
McCarthy, Gail, "Literacy Mission Continues at the Sawyer Library," *Gloucester Daily Times*, January 20, 2008, <https://www.gloucestertimes.com/news/local_news/literacy-mission-continues-at-the-sawyer-library/article_aa5ab4ae-71a7-5643-991f-29638c72039b.html>
"Portraits of Cape Ann Immigrants," Sawyer Free Library, Gloucester, MA, November 14–December 31, 2019.
Reeve, Catherine, "Vehicle for Change," *Chicago Tribune*, March 14, 1993, <https://www.gloucestertimes.com/news/local_news/literacy-mission-continues-at-the-sawyer-library/article_aa5ab4ae-71a7-5643-991f-29638c72039b.html>
Shetterly, Robert, *Americans Who Tell the Truth* (New York: Dutton, 2005).

Times Staff, "Celebrating Fishermen's Wives," *Gloucester Daily Times*, August 6, 2021, <https://www.gloucestertimes.com/news/fishing_industry_news/celebrating-fishermens-wives/article_0a340621-a74c-5f82-b545-00fb185efbda.html>

Zappone, Katherine, "We Love This Place," in *Choosing the Future II, Proceedings of a Symposium*, Gloucester, MA, January 19–20, 1996.

Chapter 11: The Lights Go Out

Anderson, Bendix, "Nightmare at Pond View Village," *Affordable Housing Finance*, January 1, 2008, <https://www.housingfinance.com/news/nightmare-at-pond-view-village_0>

Dalmau, Tim, and Bernie Neville, *Olympus Inc: Intervening for Cultural Change in Organizations* (Abingdon, England: Routledge, 2019).

Dean, Mike, "Slump in Condo Sales Puts Heralded Project in Default with Main Lender," *Gloucester Daily Times*, <https://www.gloucestertimes.com/news/local_news/slump-in-condo-sales-puts-heralded-project-in-default-with-main-lender/article_b9f5121b-daca-5966-9b72-3a8e5b2905a7.html>

Dwyer, Ciara, "Ann and Katherine Say It Loud," *Irish Independent*, October 18, 2008, <https://www.independent.ie/style/sex-relationships/ann-and-katherine-say-it-loud/26486166.html>

Knowles, Richard N., *The Leadership Dance: Pathways to Extraordinary Organizational Effectiveness* (St Petersburg, FL: Center for Self-Organizing Leadership, 2002).

Kunreuther, Frances, and Stephanie Clohesy, *The Long Goodbye: Advice, How-Tos, and Cautionary Tales for Extended Leadership Exits* (New York: Building Movement Project, 2016).

McMahon, Katie, "Key Housing Site Facing Foreclosure," *Gloucester Daily Times*, July 14, 2008, <https://www.gloucestertimes.com/news/local_news/key-housing-site-facing-foreclosure-acclaimed-caho-project-property-going-up-for-auction/article_739e9914-7bc3-5297-b09b-01edd4935958.html>

Mullally, Una, *In the Name of Love: The Movement for Marriage Equality in Ireland* (Dublin: The History Press Ireland, 2014).

Tuomala, Jari, Donald Yeh, and Katie Smith Milway, "Making Founder Successions Work," *Stanford Social Innovation Review* (Spring 2018), <https://ssir.org/articles/entry/making_founder_successions_work>

Epilogue: The Power of Mutuality

Hollins, Ben, and Charlotte Hollins, *The Fight for Fordhall Farm* (London: Hodder & Stoughton, 2007).
Wresinki, Joseph, *The Very Poor, Living Proof of the Indivisibility of Human Rights* (Paris: French Commission on Human Rights, 1989).
"Redefining Human Rights-Based Development: The Wresinski Approach to Partnership with the Poorest," United Nations Division for Social Policy and Development Department of Economic and Social Affairs, December 1999.
Sheldrake, Merlin, *Entangled Life: How Fungi Make Our Worlds, Change Our Minds & Shape Our Futures* (New York: Random House, 2020).

About the Authors

CHUCK COLLINS is an activist and author of numerous books, including *Born on Third Base, Wealth and Our Commonwealth* (with Bill Gates Sr), and a new novel, *Altar to an Erupting Sun*. Collins is director of the Program on Inequality and the Common Good at the Institute for Policy Studies, where he co-edits Inequality.org.

KIMBERLY FRENCH writes essays and journalism, which have appeared in journals such as *Salon, Utne Reader, Tikkun, Brain, Child, Nieman Reports, Boston Globe Sunday Magazine, Natural New England,* and *UU World,* where she was a long-time contributing editor. Her works have been nominated for a Pushcart Prize and listed twice as Notable Essays in the *Best American Essays* series. Also an activist, she founded a local nonprofit in her town that educates and advocates for policies to help low/moderate-income households transition to clean energy.

ROSEMARY HAUGHTON and NANCY SCHWOYER are two of the founders of Wellspring House in Gloucester, Massachusetts, and lived and worked there for more than thirty years. Together, they have led conferences and retreats, given talks on progressive topics, and published numerous articles and papers.

ROSEMARY HAUGHTON began writing while raising a large family, publishing more than thirty books on religion, family, and theology. She has written many articles and longer papers on these subjects, specifically about the theology and spirituality of hospitality. She also illustrated some of her own and other books. She has lectured widely in England, Australia, Canada, the United States, and other countries, and worked with the World Council of Churches at a conference in Romania. She has no formal degrees but has received three honorary degrees and many other awards.

NANCY SCHWOYER has always been an educator and has created innovative secondary-school programs as well as adult education and comprehensive parish education programs. She wrote and taught a women's history course at Wellspring's Community Education Center. She has been deeply involved in the civil-rights, women's, and peace movements, as well as advocacy for affordable housing, shelter, and anti-poverty policy. She has a bachelor's degree in communication arts from St Mary-of-the-Woods College in Indiana and a master's in English literature from the University of North Carolina at Chapel Hill. She has also done postgraduate work in theology and education at Boston College and earned a Certificate of Advanced Education Specialization (CAES).

www.ingramcontent.com/pod-product-compliance
Ingram Content Group UK Ltd.
Pitfield, Milton Keynes, MK11 3LW, UK
UKHW021313180426
11947UKWH00015B/1197